BULLIED

Joe Osborne

www.dizzyemupublishing.com

DIZZY EMU PUBLISHING

1714 N McCadden Place, Hollywood, Los Angeles 90028

www.dizzyemupublishing.com

Bullied

Joe Osborne

ISBN-13: 978-1537529417

First published in the United States

in 2016 by Dizzy Emu Publishing

www.dizzyemupublishing.com

Bullied

Joe Osborne

EXT. SOCCER FIELD EARLY MORNING

A truck backs slowly into frame and two people get out and
begin to unload white folding chairs on to the field.

                    KURTIS
               (voice over)
          Moving from a big city to a small
          town like beaver falls took some
          getting used to. Beaver falls is a
          quiet community, population
          hovering around 5,000 but whether
          the population is 50,000 or 500 one
          thing seems to be a constant, High
          school will leave its mark on all
          of us.

The men start aligning the chairs in rows and then a podium
is unloaded and placed to the left of the chairs.

                    KURTIS
               (Voice Over)
          I moved to this town looking for a
          new identity, to find out who I am.
          The lessons I have learned will
          stay with me forever like Sometimes
          your actions no matter how small
          have real consequences and the
          echoes of a painful past can haunt
          us. Can you rise above it before it
          breaks your character. Sometimes no
          matter how strong you are the fight
          is just too much to take. Tom
          helped me find who I was, this is
          his story which will no doubt be
          twisted and misconstrued by those
          who were not there but I was there
          so let's start at the beginning.

EXT. PARK DAY

Young Tom and his mom pull up and park. Tom looks nervous.

                    TOM
          I don't know anyone here, why can't
          I just go with you and dad?

                    MRS. LEWISTON
          This is how you'll meet new
          friends, besides you don't want to
          be stuck in some boring office
          while me and your dad sign some
          papers for the house.

                                              (CONTINUED)

                    TOM
          Yeah I guess you are right.

                    MRS. LEWISTON
          Plus look, there is your cousin
          John.

Tom gets out of the car and waves as his mom pulls away.

Tom sits there for a moment then sees his cousin is being
picked on by a bigger kid.

Tom walks over to see what's going on.

The big kid named Glen and his friends have taken John's
glasses and passing them around.

                    JOHN
          Come on, I can't see without those.

                    GLEN
          Reach for them, haha oh, you almost
          got em.

                    TOM
          Hey!

Glen passes the glasses off and turns to face Tom.

                    GLEN
          What do you want small fry?

                    TOM
          Give him his glasses back.

                    GLEN
          What's it to you?

                    TOM
          It's not nice to pick on people.

                    GLEN
          OOH did you hear that guys, it
          isn't nice, ha ha.

                    TOM
          Just leave him alone.

                    GLEN
          Or you could mind your own
          business, unless you want to get
          beat up.

                                        (CONTINUED)

                              TOM
                    He's my Cousin.

Glen looks at John then back at Tom

                              GLEN
                    Wow, it makes sense now i can see
                    the resemblance. You are both small
                    and weak looking.

Glen gets in Tom's face, clearly the bigger of the two.

                              TOM
                    Can't we just all get along and be
                    friends?

Glen pushes Tom backwards and laughs.

                              GLEN
                    Friends? you and me?

                              TOM
                    yeah.

                              GLEN
                    why would I want to be friends with
                    you loser?

                              TOM
                    I am not a loser.

                              GLEN
                    I think you are, I don't even think
                    your own parents want you.

Tom's eyes start to water.

                              GLEN
                    Ah, little baby gonna cry?

Glen gets in Tom's face

                              GLEN
                    You gonna say something?

Tom stands silent

                              GLEN
                    That's what I thought.

Tom turns to walk away, Glen kicks his feet and trips him.

Tom falls on his face and has a bloody nose and scrapes his
elbow.

                    TOM
          Why did you do that?

                    GLEN
          I didn't do anything guess you just
          have bad balance loser.

Tom turns and runs towards his aunt's car that has just
arrived.

John follows close behind.

                    CHARLOTTE
          Tom, oh my god what happened to
          you.

Tom runs past her and just sits in the car.

                    CHARLOTTE
          Well what happened John?

                    JOHN
          Some bully was picking on me and
          Tom tried to help.

                    CHARLOTTE
          Are you hurt too?

                    JOHN
          They took my glasses and they
          wouldn't give them back. They
          broke.

                    CHARLOTTE
          Who did this?

John points to Glen and his group of friends.

                    JOHN
          His name is Glen, He's older then
          us and big.

                    CHARLOTTE
          Well maybe I should have a talk
          with his parents.

                    JOHN
          No, mom he'll just pick on us more.

                    CHARLOTTE
          Well you should just stay away from
          him, are you alright?

(CONTINUED)

                         JOHN
               Yeah, I'm alright.

John and his mom get in the car and drive away from the
park.

a few minutes of driving go by in silence, Tom's bloody nose
is caking over and his are red from crying.

                         CHARLOTTE
               Tom, how are you doing back there?

Charlotte looks in the rear view mirror to see Tom looking
at the floor.

The car pulls up to Tom's house, a long dirt driveway.

Tom rushes out of the car running towards the house.

Charlotte get's out to talk to her sister.

                         MRS. LEWISTON
               Tom, hey what's wrong sweetie?

Tom runs passed his mother and into the house tears in his
eyes.

                         MRS. LEWISTON
               What was that all about?

                         CHARLOTTE
               John was getting picked on by
               bullies and i guess Tom tried to
               help. I asked him but He was silent
               the whole ride over.

                         MRS. LEWISTON
               Alright, well thank you for
               bringing him home, I'll try to see
               what happened.

                         CHARLOTTE
               Alright sis, I really hope he's
               okay.

                         MRS. LEWISTON
               I'll let you know, how's John?

                         CHARLOTTE
               He's fine, He broke his glasses.

                                              (CONTINUED)

                              MRS. LEWISTON
                    That's too bad, well thank you so
                    much for bringing Tom home.

                              CHARLOTTE
                    Of course, I hope He's alright.

                              MRS. LEWISTON
                    I'll call you.

                              CHARLOTTE
                    Alright.

Charlotte rolls up the car window and backs the car out of
the driveway waving goodbye to Mrs. Lewiston.

Mrs. Lewiston waves back then turns to the house and lets
out a sigh.

INT TOM'S KITCHEN AFTERNOON

Mrs. Lewiston enters the house to find Tom Sitting on the
couch looking out the window.

                              MRS. LEWISTON
                    Tom?

Tom turns around to look at his mom

Tom's mom sits on the couch next to him.

                              MRS. LEWISTON
                    You want to tell me what happened
                    today?

Tom shakes his head

                              MRS. LEWISTON
                    Will you let me see your face?

Tom turns his face into the light showing his face which is
scratched and dried blood is trailing from his nose.

                              MRS. LEWISTON
                    Your aunt Charlotte tells me you
                    had problems with a bigger kid
                    today.

Tom nods his head

                                                    (CONTINUED)

                              MRS. LEWISTON
                    So you were trying to help your
                    cousin?

                              TOM
                    They took his glasses so i asked
                    them to nicely give them back.

                              MRS. LEWISTON
                    Did they?

                              TOM
                    no.

                              MRS. LEWISTON
                    How did your face get hurt? did you
                    fight with him?

                              TOM
                    No I turned to walk away and the
                    big kid kicked my feet and i fell.

Mrs. Lewiston hugs Tom

                              MRS. LEWISTON
                    Well you're safe here.

Tom breaks the hug and looks up at his mom.

                              MRS. LEWISTON
                    Is something wrong Tom?

                              TOM
                    Do you and dad love me?

                              MRS. LEWISTON
                    Of course we do, why would you ask
                    that?

                              TOM
                    The bully said you and dad were
                    embarrassed to be my parents and
                    you don't like me.

Mrs. Lewiston holds Tom's face toward her and looks him in
the eyes.

                              MRS. LEWISTON
                    Hey look at me, are you listening?
                    I love you more then anything in
                    the world and me and your father
                    will love you and always be proud
                    of you no matter what alright.

(CONTINUED)

                         TOM
               Alright mommy.

Mrs. Lewiston gives him a big hug and holds him there for a
few moments.

                         MRS. LEWISTON
               We should get you cleaned up.

Mrs. Lewiston walks into the bathroom run's the faucet
shortly and comes back with a wet rag and peroxide.

                         MRS. LEWISTON
               Here, look up.

Tom looks up at his mom.

Mrs. Lewiston cleans his bloody nose

                         MRS. LEWISTON
               Did you hurt anything else?

                         TOM
               Yeah, my elbow.

Tom shows his mom his elbow.

Mrs. Lewiston dips her rag in peroxide.

                         MRS. LEWISTON
               This might sting a little.

Mrs. Lewiston puts the rag with peroxide on Tom's elbow.

Tom winces slightly.

                         MRS. LEWISTON
               All done, that wasn't so bad was
               it.

Tom shakes his head

                         MRS. LEWISTON
               Lay down and get some rest, I'll
               wake you up for dinner.

Tom lays down on the couch

Mrs. Lewiston kisses him on the forehead.

                         MRS. LEWISTON
               I will always love you Tom.

Tom looks out the window and watches as the sun sets.

Tom shuts his eyes and falls asleep.

INT. KITCHEN NIGHT

Tom can hear his mom in the kitchen and his dad walking
around, his eyes are still closed.

> MRS. LEWISTON
> Tom, hey dinner's almost ready you
> should go wash up.

Tom opens his eyes, yawns and stretches.

Tom heads to the bathroom and flips on the light.

Tom opens his eyes wide and scrunches his nose which hurts
from his fall. He turns the faucet on and washes his hands.

Tom turns the faucet off and slowly makes his way to the
kitchen table.

> MRS. LEWISTON
> Hey there sleepyhead.

Tom yawns.

> TOM
> What's for dinner?

> MRS. LEWISTON
> Your favorite Mac n' cheese

Tom perks up and smiles.

> TOM
> Alright!

> MRS. LEWISTON
> I thought you might like that.

Mr. Lewiston walks in the kitchen.

> MR. LEWISTON
> Hey kiddo, how was your day.

> TOM
> It was okay.

> MRS. LEWISTON
> How was your first day of work?

(CONTINUED)

                                    MR. LEWISTON
                              Ugh, could have gone better.

Mr. Lewiston walks to the freezer pulling out a bag of ice
and putting ice cubes in a small glass and pouring Jamesons
whiskey and takes a sip.

                                    MRS. LEWISTON
                              That bad huh?

Mr. Lewiston takes a deep sigh.

                                    MR. LEWISTON
                              Yeah.

Mrs. Lewiston kisses Mr. Lewiston on the cheek.

                                    MRS. LEWISTON
                              I'm sorry hon, give it time, this
                              will work out.

Mr. Lewiston takes another sip of his whiskey.

                                    MR. LEWISTON
                              Yeah, I'm glad you're so confident.

Mr. Lewiston walks to the table to sit and notices Tom
slumping with his head down.

                                    MR. LEWISTON
                              Hey bud, are you alright? let me
                              see you.

                                    MRS. LEWISTON
                              He really had a long day..

                                    MR. LEWISTON
                              Can you just let him answer me damn
                              it!

Tom turns his head and his father can see his scratch on his
face.

                                    MR. LEWISTON
                              What happened to you?

                                    TOM
                              I saw John getting picked on at the
                              park and I tried to help but the
                              big kid pushed me down.

                         MR. LEWISTON
          Did you fight back?

                              TOM
          No sir.

                         MR. LEWISTON
          You should have.

                              MRS. LEWISTON
          Henry!

                         MR. LEWISTON
          What? I'm Telling him to stand up
          for himself. Look at me Tom.

Tom looks at his father

                         MR. LEWISTON
          If you let that kid push you around
          you will be a door mat you're whole
          life, trust me, put him down and he
          will leave you alone.

                         MRS. LEWISTON
          Oh that's just great.

                         MR. LEWISTON
          What? Teaching him to not get
          walked all over and maybe he won't
          be like me in a shit job at the
          bottom of the barrel.

                         MRS. LEWISTON
          Well I don't want him thinking
          violence is just the go to answer.

                         MR. LEWISTON
          Why, My father told me to fight for
          what I believe in and never give
          up.

Mrs. Lewiston scoffs

                         MR. LEWISTON
          What was that?

                         MRS. LEWISTON
          Oh nothing, I just think maybe you
          should quote a better role model.

Mr. Lewiston is clearly offended but says nothing and
refills his glass of whiskey.

Tom is clearly getting uncomfortable.

                    MRS. LEWISTON
          Here you go Tom.

Mrs. Lewiston hands Tom a bowl of Macaroni and Cheese

                    TOM
          Do we have any crazy Jane?

                    MRS. LEWISTON
          Let me check.

Mrs. Lewiston checks the spice rack and pulls out Crazy Jane
and hands it to Tom.

                    TOM
          Sweet, thanks mom.

                    MRS. LEWISTON
          You're welcome sweetie.

                    MR. LEWISTON
              (Sarcastically)
          Oh joy Mac and cheese, my favorite.

                    MRS. LEWISTON
              (Sarcastically)
          Oh, really? that's good we can have
          it everyday then.

Tom eats a few big bites sensing some tension in the room.

Mr. Lewiston Slams his fist on the table.

                    MR. LEWISTON
          My dad was a good man! He did right
          by me and my mom.

                    MRS. LEWISTON
          That's a joke, He treated you and
          your mom and you like shit.

Mr. Lewiston stands up and walks to fill his glass of
whiskey.

                    MRS. LEWISTON
          I guess He taught you that too huh?

                    MR. LEWISTON
          What the hell does that mean?

                         MRS. LEWISTON
                    Face it, your father was a drunk
                    and a abusive ass.

                         MR. LEWISTON
                    SHUT UP!

Mr. Lewiston slaps Mrs. Lewiston hard knocking her back into
the fridge.

Tom starts to feel scared.

Mr. Lewiston shuts his eyes in regret.

Mrs. Lewiston stands there in shock for a moment.

                         MRS. LEWISTON
                    There you go, show me what kind of
                    man you are.

Tom gets up from the table scared and runs to his room.

                         MR. LEWISTON
                    Tom, wait.

                         MRS. LEWISTON
                    A great way to show our son how to
                    treat a woman.

                         MR. LEWISTON
                    I'm so

                         MRS. LEWISTON
                    Don't, I don't want to hear I'm
                    sorry right now.

Mrs. Lewiston Leaves the room

Mr. Lewiston leans up against the counter and sighs putting
his head down in shame.

EXT. TOMS BACKYARD DAY

Tom sits in the yard with his head looking at the ground.

The phone rings, Mrs. Lewiston answers it.

                         MRS. LEWISTON
                    Hello?

                              CHARLOTTE
                    Hey sis, how are you?

                              MRS. LEWISTON
                    I've been better, Henry's job is
                    stressing him out which is
                    stressing me out.

                              CHARLOTTE
                    Aw, that's not good.

                              MRS. LEWISTON
                    Not at all, Tom saw us fighting
                    last week. Henry started drinking
                    again pretty heavy.

                              CHARLOTTE
                    How is Tom doing? I was thinking
                    about him the other day.

                              MRS. LEWISTON
                    I'm worried about him Charlotte, He
                    just sits in the backyard and looks
                    so sad.

                              CHARLOTTE
                    Yeah I know what you mean, I can't
                    get John to go out and play or go
                    back to the park. He says He is
                    afraid of that Glen kid.

                              MRS. LEWISTON
                    I wish I knew some way to get him
                    back and playing.

                              CHARLOTTE
                    Well I know John won't go back
                    unless Tom is there.

                              MRS. LEWISTON
                    I'll ask him again but I don't
                    think he'll go.

                              MRS. LEWISTON
                    Tom, come here a second.

Tom looks up and heads over to his mom.

Mrs. Lewiston pulls the phone away from her mouth.

                              TOM
                    Yeah mom?

                        MRS. LEWISTON
            You look a little bored buddy.

                        TOM
            Yeah I guess a little.

                        MRS. LEWISTON
            Would you want to see your cousin?

                        TOM
            Yeah that would be cool.

                        MRS. LEWISTON
            Well your aunt is trying to get him
            to go back to the park and He won't
            go unless you go.

Tom loses his excitement

                        TOM
            Oh, can't he just come over here?

                        MRS. LEWISTON
             Buddy are you scared you'll get
            picked on by Glen again?

                        TOM
            Maybe a little.

                        MRS. LEWISTON
            You and John just stay away from
            him.

                        TOM
            I don't know

                        MRS. LEWISTON
            Please Tom do this for me? Me and
            your aunt need some sister time.

                        TOM
            Alright I guess.

Mrs. Lewiston kisses him on the forehead.

                        MRS. LEWISTON
            Thank you honey, it will be alright
            and I'll be there to pick you up in
            a bit.

                        TOM
            Alright mom, I'm going to get my
            hat.

                              MRS. LEWISTON
                    Alright I'll start the car.

Mrs. Lewiston puts the phone back to her mouth.

                              MRS. LEWISTON
                    Charlotte?

                              CHARLOTTE
                    Yeah I'm here Sue

                              MRS. LEWISTON
                    I convinced Tom to go to the park,
                    would you want to grab some coffee?

                              CHARLOTTE
                    Oh that's great, yeah I'd love to.

                              MRS. LEWISTON
                    Alright I will see you soon.

                              CHARLOTTE
                    Sounds good, see ya.

Tom comes back outside and gets in the car.

Mrs. Lewiston turns the car on and backs it down the drive
way.

                              MRS. LEWISTON
                    It will be alright, you'll see.

EXT. PARK DAY

Tom pulls up in the car and gets out but doesn't walk into
the play area yet, He turns and looks at his mom.

                              MRS. LEWISTON
                    Just remember what I said, stay
                    away from Glen and have fun with
                    your cousin.

                              TOM
                    I'll try.

Mrs. Lewiston drives away and Tom walks over to his cousin.

                              TOM
                    Hey John.

                         JOHN
               Hey, how are you?

                         TOM
               I've been bored but a little scared
               to be back here.

                         JOHN
               I know the feeling. So what do you
               wanna do?

                         TOM
               I don't know, do you want to play
               Hacky Sack?

                         JOHN
               Yeah, that sounds fun.

                         TOM
               Hey, where are your glasses?

                         JOHN
               I left them at home just in case
               Glen bothered us.

                         TOM
               Good thinking.

Tom pulls out a hacky sack and throws it to john

John kicks it to Tom who kicks it up high in the air.

                         JOHN
               I got it.

John runs back and just barely gets it back to Tom

Tom stalls it and kicks it back to John.

Tom and John are laughing and comfortable.

John kicks the hacky sack hard and it flies past Tom and
hits Glen.

                         GLEN
               Hey, what the.

                         TOM
               Oh no.

Glen turns around to see Tom and John

                              GLEN
                    Well well, what do we have here?

                              JOHN
                    Can we just have our hacky sack
                    back.

                              GLEN
                    You hit me with it.

                              JOHN
                    It was just an accident

                              GLEN
                    I don't think it was, I think you
                    did on purpose.

Glen starts to step towards John

Tom steps in front of John.

                              TOM
                    Just let it go Glen

                              GLEN
                    And if I don't?

Glen takes a step closer to Tom

                              GLEN
                    Are you gonna do something? Huh?

The noises start to fade and Tom can hear his dads voice.

                              MR. LEWISTON
                         (Voice Over)
                    Remember son, if you let them once
                    they will walk all over you your
                    whole life. Stand up and fight,
                    take a breath, dig your feet and
                    don't give them an inch. Let them
                    know you will not be shoved around.

the sounds of the world fade back in.

                              GLEN
                    I said what are you going to do
                    about it punk.

Tom screams and pushes Glen back and he falls into dog shit.

Glen's friends chuckle a little.

                                                        (CONTINUED)

                         GLEN
              Shut up!

                         TOM
              Leave us alone!

Glens friends help him off the ground.

                         GLEN
              Oh you are going to get it, you
              hear me? you are going to get it.

Glen and his friends start walking away

                         TOM
              Yeah walk away.

John stands there looking stunned.

                         JOHN
              Tom, that was awesome.

                         TOM
              My dad told me to stand up for
              myself.

                         JOHN
              I wish I had that.

                         TOM
              Don't you have a dad.

                         JOHN
              My mom says he died when I was
              born.

                         TOM
              Sorry to hear that man

                         JOHN
              It's alright I guess, so what do
              you want to do.

                         TOM
              I don't know.

                         JOHN
              We could play in the woods.

                         TOM
              Yeah, we just have to watch out for
              bigfoot.

                         JOHN
          What's bigfoot?

                         TOM
          Walk with me, I'll tell you.

Tom and John walk off into the woods.

EXT. PARK LATE AFTERNOON

John and Tom are walking through the woods hours later
discussing and looking for big foot clues.

                         JOHN
          So they think this creature is
          living around here?

                         TOM
          I haven't heard of any being seen
          but they like the woods.

John Checks his watch.

                         JOHN
          Oh man.

                         TOM
          What?

                         JOHN
          We have to go, it's time to meet my
          mom.

                         TOM
          Let's go I'll race you

Tom and John sprint off and come out of the woods towards
the parking lot where John's mom is waiting by the car.

                         CHARLOTTE
          There you boys are.

                         JOHN
          Sorry mom me and Tom were running
          around in the woods.

                         CHARLOTTE
          So you had fun today? No trouble
          from Glen?

                         JOHN
               No, Tom was so brave mom you should
               have seen it.

                         CHARLOTTE
               What does that mean.

                         JOHN
               He was picking on us and Tom
               knocked him over and he left us
               alone it was so awesome.

                         CHARLOTTE
               I don't like that, you should have
               just walked away.

                         TOM
               But my dad said not to back and
               down and run away.

Charlotte sighs.

                         CHARLOTTE
               Alright well I'm giving you a ride
               home tonight, let's pile in.

Tom and John and Charlotte get into the car.

                         CHARLOTTE
               Seat belts.

Charlotte drives to Toms house.

Tom gets out of the car and turns to say goodbye to his
aunt.

                         TOM
               Thank you for the right Aunty
               Charlotte.

                         CHARLOTTE
               Your welcome, we'll see you next
               week on the fourth.

                         TOM
               Alright that sounds awesome, see ya
               John.

                         JOHN
               See ya, and thanks for standing up
               for me today.

                              TOM
                    Anytime man.

Tom heads inside the house and Charlotte leaves.

EXT. TOM'S BACKYARD AFTERNOON

Tom's father has the grill open and cooking burgers and hot
dogs.

Mrs. Lewiston and Charlotte are drink Margaritas and Mrs.
Lewiston brings Henry a beer.

                              MRS. LEWISTON
                    Here you go honey.

Henry takes a swig of his beer.

                              MR. LEWISTON
                    Thanks Jenny, how are you today
                    Charlotte.

                              CHARLOTTE
                    I'm doing good, Thanks for inviting
                    us today. John is really happy to
                    hang out with Tom.

                              MRS. LEWISTON
                    Our pleasure sis. How is John doing
                    lately.

                              CHARLOTTE
                    It's been really good for him to
                    have Tom.

                              MRS. LEWISTON
                    He's such a good kid and Tom is
                    adjusting to the move better having
                    someone to hang out with.

                              CHARLOTTE
                    They sure are growing up quick, I
                    remember the last time I saw Tom he
                    was just a little guy.

                              MRS. LEWISTON
                    Yeah Seems like it was just
                    yesterday I was watching him take
                    his first steps, now he's running
                    around and going into middle
                    school.

                                              (CONTINUED)

                    CHARLOTTE
          I know, John is growing up quick,
          he's starting to ask difficult
          questions.

Charlotte takes a sip of her Margarita and puts her head
down.

                    MR. LEWISTON
          What kind of questions?

                    CHARLOTTE
          Questions about his father and I
          know this day was coming eventually
          but I still don't know what to say
          to him.

                    MRS. LEWISTON
          Oh I am sorry Charlotte. Do you
          know where his father is?

                    CHARLOTTE
          No, it was one of those heat of the
          moment one night things. You know
          aided by one fifty one shots.

                    MRS. LEWISTON
          What a Jerk, I bet He's married or
          something.

                    CHARLOTTE
          Either way, Having John was the
          most amazing gift and I wouldn't
          change that for a minute.

                    MR. LEWISTON
          He really is a good kid.

                    MRS. LEWISTON
          And you are a doing an amazing job
          with him on your own.

Mrs. Lewiston Hugs Charlotte who is tearing up a little

                    MR. LEWISTON
          Where are those two anyway food is
          almost ready.

                    MRS. LEWISTON
          I think they were running around in
          the woods.

                         MR. LEWISTON
              Tom! John! time to come back now
              the food is ready.

Tom and John come running around the other side of the house
laughing and pushing each other.

Tom tries to catch his breath.

                         TOM
              Hey dad

                         MR. LEWISTON
              Hey pal, where were you two.

                         TOM
              Just running around in the woods.

                         MR. LEWISTON
              Looking for that foot thing?

                         TOM
              Bigfoot dad.

Mr. Lewiston laughs and pats Tom on the head.

                         MR. LEWISTON
              You kids crack me up, are you boys
              hungry?

                         TOM
              Yeah starving.

                         MR. LEWISTON
              Good because food is ready, do you
              want hot dogs or cheeseburgers?

                         TOM
              Can I have both?

                         MR. LEWISTON
              Sure you can, and John how about
              you?

                         JOHN
              Same please uncle Henry.

                         MR. LEWISTON
              You got it.

                         MRS. LEWISTON
              You kids be careful running around
              these woods, I don't want anything
              bad to happen to you.

                                              (CONTINUED)

                    JOHN
          We're careful mom, besides Bigfoot
          aren't dangerous.

                    MRS. LEWISTON
          It's not the Bigfoot we're worried
          about out there.

                    TOM
          Then what?

                    MR. LEWISTON
          Wolves, snakes, even bears can be
          dangerous if you get too close to a
          cub or spook them and Humans.

                    MRS. LEWISTON
          Just always stick to the trails.

                    TOM
          Alright mom we will, promise.

                    JOHN
          Wow Bears are my favorite animals.

                    CHARLOTTE
          I know honey but just admire them
          from a distance, they are very
          powerful animals.

                    JOHN
          we will keep our distance.

                    CHARLOTTE
          Good, thank you.

                    TOM
          When do the fireworks start?

                    MR. LEWISTON
          Should be very soon, the suns
          sinking now.

                    TOM
          Happy Labor day dad.

                    MR. LEWISTON
          Happy Labor day buddy.

They all sit in the lawn chairs and eat as the sun goes
down.

The fireworks start and Tom and John watch on excitedly.

INT TOMS ROOM NIGHT

Mrs. Lewiston tucks Tom into bed and John is set up in a
sleeping bag on the bed beside getting settled.

>   TOM
>   Wow that was awesome, I love the
>   fireworks show. I think my favorite
>   is the green one.

Mrs. Lewiston laughs and covers him up.

>   MRS. LEWISTON
>   Alright, it's time to lay down.
>   It's late.

>   TOM
>   Aw but we're not tired, are we
>   John?

John Yawns.

>   JOHN
>   Nope, not even a little.

Charlotte and Henry walk into the room.

>   MR. LEWISTON
>   What's going on here, do we have
>   non sleepers?

>   MRS. LEWISTON
>   Yeah, I'm afraid so

Henry moves over to Tom's bed.

Tom starts laughing.

>   MR. LEWISTON
>   That my friend has a consequence.

>   MRS. LEWISTON
>   Really what would that be?

>   MR. LEWISTON
>   Well.. that is a tickling offense.

Henry starts tickling Tom

Tom laughs and squirms.

(CONTINUED)

                         TOM
             Alright, Alirght, I'll sleep

Henry laughs and covers Tom.

                         MR. LEWISTON
             Alright Buddy, get some sleep.

                         TOM
             Goodnight Dad, Goodnight Mom, Good
             night Aunt Charlotte.

                         MRS. LEWISTON
             Goodnight Tom, Goodnight John.

                         JOHN
             Goodnight Aunt Julie, Goodnight
             Mom, Good night uncle Henry.

                         MR. LEWISTON
             Goodnight John

                         CHARLOTTE
             Goodnight honey.

Mrs. Lewiston, Mr. Lewiston and Charlotte leave the room

                         TOM
             Today was fun wasn't it John?

John is snoring.

Tom lays on his side and nods off.

Hours later Tom starts rolling from side to side

                         TOM
             No!

Tom continues to thrash in his sleep

sounds of Terrified teens start to be heard

Tom begins to sweat and thrash more knocking his pillow off
on to John

                         JOHN
             Huh? Tom?

John sits up and sees Tom thrashing and walks to him.

                         TOM
                No, Wait. Don't

                         JOHN
                Tom? Wake up man.

Tom starts yelling louder.

INT SCHOOL DAY

Tom can hear a school bell ring then a loud gunshot.

Kids are running scared in slow motion and screaming

Tom tries to talk to them.

                         TOM
                Hey wait what's wrong?

                         TOM
                Where am I?

                         TOM
                Can't you hear me?

No one responds to him as he continues down the hall more
shots go off.

Tom ducks into the bathroom to hide. He slowly backs toward
the window keeping his eye on the door.

More gunshots ring out.

Tom can hear his name being called by John and his Mom
Echoing.

Tom slowly Turns toward the mirror and sees someone older
and blood covered face smiling.

One last gunshot rings out then Black.

 INT TOMS ROOM NIGHT

Tom screaming shoots straight up

Mrs. Lewiston grabs Tom

                         MRS. LEWISTON
                Tom, hey it's alright now.

Tom still shaking stops screaming and tries to catch his
breathe.

                                              (CONTINUED)

Mrs. Lewiston rubs his hair and holds him

John looks on in fear and concern

Henry sits at the edge of the bed.

Charlotte stands in the doorway.

                       MRS. LEWISTON
                  (Softly)
          Shh. you're alright now.

                       TOM
         It was awful mom.

                       MR. LEWISTON
         It was just a nightmare champ. I
         know they're scary.

                       TOM
         It felt so real, I could hear
         screaming.

                       MR. LEWISTON
         Screaming?

                       TOM
         Yeah, I was at a school but I was
         not me, I was older and had blood
         on my face.

Henry and Julie exchange looks of concern.

Julie hugs Tom

                       MRS. LEWISTON
         Well you're awake and safe now.

                       MR. LEWISTON
         Dreams can seem real but they can't
         hurt you son, now try and lay back
         down.

Mrs. Lewiston tucks Tom back into bed.

Julie, Charlotte, and Henry slowly leave the room

                       TOM
         Hey mom?

Julie steps back in.

                        MRS. LEWISTON
          Yeah?

                        TOM
          Can you leave the light hall light
          on?

                        MRS. LEWISTON
          Sure buddy.

Julie leaves the door open halfway and clicks the bedroom
light off leaving the hall light.

Tom lays there staring at the ceiling wide awake.

                        JOHN
          Dude, that was scary

                        TOM
          You're telling me.

                        JOHN
          You wouldn't wake up, I kept
          shaking you.

                        TOM
          It was so real John, they were
          running from me.

Tom and John lay there in silence for a few minutes.

                        TOM
          What do you think it means?

                        JOHN
          What?

                        TOM
          The dream.

                        JOHN
          Maybe it was just a dream man,
          Sometimes they don't make sense.

                        TOM
          Yeah... Maybe you're right.

Tom lays there in silence thinking and looking at the
ceiling the he finally shuts his eyes.

INT TOM'S KITCHEN MORNING

Tom comes into the kitchen yawning and sits down at the
table and grabs a cup of orange juice.

                    JOHN
          Hey man you look exhausted.

                    TOM
          Yeah I did not really go back to
          sleep.

                    MRS. LEWISTON
          Do you want some eggs?

                    TOM
          No thanks, not really hungry.

                    JOHN
          First day jitters?

                    TOM
          Huh?

                    JOHN
          Today is our first day of seventh
          grade.

                    TOM
          Oh, that's right we have school.

                    JOHN
          Wow you must be tired.

                    TOM
          Hey mom did you put my new backpack
          somewhere?

                    MRS. LEWISTON
          It's on the couch, are you sure you
          don't want me to drive you your
          first day?

                    TOM
          That's alright we'll take the bus.

Tom finishes his juice and grabs his backpack and walks to
the door and stops.

John throws his backpack on and stands up

Tom takes a few deep breathes.

(CONTINUED)

                         MRS. LEWISTON
                    Is everything alright.

                         TOM
                    I don't want to do this, I'm
                    nervous.

                         MRS. LEWISTON
                    Aw don't be nervous you'll do
                    great.

                         TOM
                    What if it's like before, what if
                    no one likes me.

                         MRS. LEWISTON
                    This is a fresh start, they will
                    like you, just be yourself.

                         JOHN
                    Yeah plus you're hanging with the
                    coolest kid in school.

John strikes a pose.

Tom smirks.

                         JOHN
                    We should get going the bus will be
                    here any minute.

Tom takes one more breath and hugs his mom.

                         TOM
                    Alright, let's do this.

                         JOHN
                    That's the spirit.

Tom and John walk out the door and down the street to the
bus stop.

The bus comes rolling down the road.

INT BUS MORNING

John and Tom climb onto the bus and peer down the aisle.

Kids are throwing paper balls and listening to their music

Tom and John take an empty seat near the front

Tom sits by the window and leans his head on the glass.

                                              (CONTINUED)

Tom jumps his head up as he hears a familiar voice.

> GLEN
> Hey Fat-ass, what's up.

Tom and John turn their heads to see Glen picking on a fat kid sitting quietly by himself.

Glen tips the fat kids book.

John sighs.

Tom sinks into his seat hoping Glen won't see him.

> JOHN
> Oh great.

> TOM
> This is going to be a fun ride to school.

> GLEN
> Hey fat ass, I'm talking to you

The fat kid just looks down at his feet.

Glen pushes him and sits in the seat with him.

> JOHN
> Poor kid, no one's even helping him.

> TOM
> You are right.

Tom sits up tall and turns to Glen

> TOM
> Hey, Leave that kid alone.

Glen turns and sees Tom and grins.

> GLEN
> Well hey Tom, and you're cousin too. This will be a fun year.

> JOHN
> Why are you on this bus, I thought you were a freshmen this year.

> GLEN
> They held me back for being awesome.

                        TOM
                    (under his breath)
            Nothing to do with the fact that
            you're dumb.

                        GLEN
            What did you just say punk.

Glen gets out of his seat and starts to move towards Tom and
John.

The bus driver catches Glen

                        BUS DRIVER
            Hey! to the back of the bus you
            leave those kids alone, I'll only
            warn you once.

Glen points to Tom and John.

                        GLEN
            You guys are going to get it, when
            you least expect it.

                        BUS DRIVER
            To the back NOW!

                        GLEN
            I'm going!

Glen moves to the back of the bus and Tom turns to the fat
kid who is picking up his books.

                        TOM
            Hey, don't worry about him he's a
            jerk, my name is Tom what's yours.

The shy fat kid does not answer.

                        TOM
            Well this is John, and we'll look
            out for you.

The bus pulls up to the school.

The kids all file out of the bus

Tom and John start to walk into the school

Glen bumps past them hard.

                                              (CONTINUED)

                    GLEN
          Watch your back.

Tom looks at John.

                    TOM
          Good start so far.

                    JOHN
          Yeah.

                    TOM
          I hope we at least one class
          together.

                    JOHN
          I don't think we do, but we have
          lunch together. Didn't you get your
          schedule.

                    TOM
          No, where do I get one.

                    JOHN
          They were supposed to mail them, it
          might be because you are new, just
          go see the office.

INT OFFICE DAY

Tom walks into the office to the office lady.

                    TOM
          Hi, I'm

The office lady holds up her hand and starts to stop him
from talking and scribbles on a piece of paper.

                    TOM
          I think they forgot to give me my
          schedule.

                    OFFICE LADY
          Just have a seat right over there
          and I'll be with you in a minute.

Tom sits in a chair and waits for a few minutes

The office lady takes a call.

                                                    (CONTINUED)

                              OFFICE LADY
                    Yes, Alright sir. Bye sir.

The office lady hangs up and Tom stands up to walk over to
her.

                              TOM
                    I'm just trying to get my schedule
                    for my classes.

                              OFFICE LADY
                    You should already have them.

                              TOM
                    I'm new, I don't think they sent
                    them to me.

                              OFFICE LADY
                    It will take a minute.

The office lady clicks on her computer and stops to check
her cell phone.

Tom Waits but keeps eying the clock.

                              TOM
                    Please I don't want to be.

The Bell rings.

                              TOM
                    Late.

The office lady hands him his schedule

Tom begins to walk away.

                              OFFICE LADY
                    Hey, you need a hall pass here.

Tom takes the hall pass and leaves.

INT CLASSROOM DAY

Tom walks into the classroom and the teacher stops talking
and everyone stares at Tom.

Tom just stands there awkwardly looking around the room.

                              MRS. CALLAHAN
                    Can I help you?

                    TOM
          Yeah, um I'm looking for a Mrs.
          Cal.

                    MRS. CALLAHAN
          It's Callahan, are you Tom
          Lewiston?

                    TOM
          Yeah that's me.

                    MRS. CALLAHAN
          Congratulations on being late your
          first day, find a empty seat. I'll
          take that pass.

Tom hands her the Hall pass and finds a empty seat in the
back of the room.

                    MRS. CALLAHAN
          Well as I was saying before you
          walked in Mr. Lewiston is that we
          are having a pop quiz on percents.

Mrs. Callahan hands out the quizzes and Tom stares at his
quiz while everyone else starts scribbling down on the
paper.

                    MRS. CALLAHAN
          Tom is there a problem?

                    TOM
          I don't know percentages.

The class laughs and Tom lowers his head.

                    MRS. CALLAHAN
          I'm sure you can figure it out.

Tom picks up his pencil and struggles through the quiz and
hands it in.

                    MRS. CALLAHAN
          Alright class for the rest of the
          time please work on these
          worksheets, what you don't complete
          will be your homework.

Tom sits there staring at the paper of percentages and
trying to figure it out not completing much.

Tom raises his hand.

                                                  (CONTINUED)

                         MRS. CALLAHAN
          Yes Tom?

                         TOM
          I'm having a hard time with this.

                         MRS. CALLAHAN
          Well just try it, and I'm always
          available after class for extra
          help.

Tom spends the rest of class trying to understand the paper.

Tom gets hit by a spitball and hears snickering.

The bell rings and everyone else leaves except for Tom.

Tom walks up to Mrs. Callahan's Desk

                         TOM
          I'm still struggling with this, can
          you help me with this?

                         MRS. CALLAHAN
          Just take it home and try to do it,
          I can't help you today.

                         TOM
          But you said..

                         MRS. CALLAHAN
          Have a nice day Tom.

Mrs. Callahan gets up and leaves and the bell rings.

Tom stands there with a look of defeat on his face.

Tom puts the paper in his bag and leaves.

INT TOM'S KITCHEN AFTERNOON

Tom walks into the kitchen and plops down at the kitchen
table and puts his head down.

Mrs. Lewiston walks into the room.

                         MRS. LEWISTON
          Hey, how was the first day?

Tom keeps his head down and just groans.

                         MRS. LEWISTON
               That bad huh?

Tom looks at his mom and just nods.

                         MRS. LEWISTON
               Well tell me what happened.

                         TOM
               Well, Glen is on our bus so that
               started it, I was late for my first
               class. I got laughed at in math
               class for not understanding it. The
               lunch is terrible. English class
               was alright I guess.

                         MRS. LEWISTON
               Well what about your other classes.

                         TOM
               science is kind of boring and our
               Gym teacher is a little out of his
               mind.

                         MRS. LEWISTON
               Any homework?

                         TOM
               Yeah a math sheet on percentages.
               These kids don't like me here mom.

                         MRS. LEWISTON
               Just try your hardest on the work
               and stay after for her help.

Tom has a look of defeat on his face.

                         MRS. LEWISTON
               Look, I know this is not easy for
               you. A strange new place, new
               people but give it a chance for me
               please.

                         TOM
               Okay mom. I just feel.

Tom puts his back down.

                         TOM
               Never mind.

(CONTINUED)

                    MRS. LEWISTON
          Feel what, you can tell me.

                    TOM
          Well just feels like everyone is
          against me.

                    MRS. LEWISTON
          Hey, look at me.

Tom looks up at his mother.

                    MRS. LEWISTON
          I'll always be on your side, no
          matter what.

Tom smiles.

                    TOM
          Where's dad.

Mrs. Lewiston sighs and looks out the window.

                    MRS. LEWISTON
          I'm sure he had to stay late again.
          How about that homework.

                    TOM
          The math is making my head spin but
          I am also supposed to read.

                    MRS. LEWISTON
          Alright well I'll call you for
          dinner.

                    TOM
          Okay I'll be in my room.

Tom grabs his bag and heads to his room.

INT TOMS ROOM NIGHT

Tom is sleeping with his book in his lap.

Tom is woken up by a loud crash.

Tom squints at the clock it reads 2am

                    MRS. LEWISTON
          HENRY?

                    MR. LEWISTON
          Yeah it's me baby.

                    MRS. LEWISTON
          DON'T BABY ME, DO YOU HAVE ANY IDEA
          WHAT TIME IT IS.

                    MR. LEWISTON
          Yeah sorry about that I had to work
          late.

                    MRS. LEWISTON
          BULLSHIT! I can smell the booze
          your breath.

                    MR. LEWISTON
          STOP OVERREACTING. I work my ass
          off and when I work late and all I
          get is shit for it.

Another loud crash makes Tom wince.

Tom grabs his MP3 player and headphones to block out the
screaming.

Tom lays back with the headphones one and falls asleep
again.

INT SCHOOL DAY

Montage of Tom in class and getting picked on and the
teacher ignoring him.

                    KURTIS
                    (Voice Over)
          Tom tried his hardest to make it
          work but things were not getting
          easier, as the months went by his
          grades rapidly declined with his
          self-esteem. Things at home were
          not any better, His father was
          drunk almost nightly which sparked
          tension in the house. Tom had been
          through a lot but nothing to
          compare him for what happened when
          the fall report cards came out.

EXT TOM'S HOUSE

John and Tom get off the bus and Tom checks his mailbox.

Tom thumbs through it until he finds a letter from the school.

>   JOHN
>   What's that?

Tom lets out a deep breath which he can see.

>   TOM
>   Oh nothing, just my doom that's
>   all.

John looks at the envelope closer.

>   JOHN
>   Oh, is that your report card?

>   TOM
>   Yes, yes it is.

Tom groans.

>   JOHN
>   Come on man, how bad can it be.

>   TOM
>   Well I'm pretty sure I failed math.

>   JOHN
>   Is your mom going to be mad?

>   TOM
>   She won't be happy.

>   JOHN
>   Are things any better with your
>   dad?

>   TOM
>   No, not really.

Mrs. Lewiston helps a very sick looking Henry into the car and backs down the driveway and rolls down the window.

>   TOM
>   Hey mom, what's going on? What's
>   wrong with dad?

(CONTINUED)

                          MRS. LEWISTON
                Tom listen to me, your father is
                sick and I'm taking him to a
                special place for him to get
                better. You're gonna stay with your
                aunt Charlotte, listen to her and
                be good alright.

                          TOM
                Alright but mom something came in
                the mail today.

                          MRS. LEWISTON
                I gotta go, be good alright love
                ya.

Mrs. Lewiston rolls the window up and takes off down the
road.

                          JOHN
                What was that all about?

                          TOM
                I have no Idea.

Charlotte pulls up and the boys get in the car.

They drive to the next street over and pull into John's
driveway. The boys get out of the car.

                          JOHN
                You know mom we could have walked.

                          CHARLOTTE
                Well I figured I would pick you up
                because it's cold.

Tom, John and Charlotte go inside the house.

INT JOHN'S DINING ROOM DUSK

Tom and John are sitting at the dining room table with
envelopes containing their report cards.

They both open them and look at them.

Tom slumps in his seat and drops the paper on the table

John shrugs his shoulders.

                        JOHN
              I did alright, no F's at least. How
              did you do? Was it as bad as you
              thought?

                        TOM
              Two F's, Math and Science.

The phone rings.

                        CHARLOTTE
              Hello? Oh hey Julie, yeah he's
              right here.

Charlotte brings the phone in the room to Tom.

                        CHARLOTTE
              Hey Tom, It's your mom.

                        TOM
              Hi mom.

                        MRS. LEWISTON
              Hey, just called to check in. How
              are things?

                        TOM
              Okay I guess, is dad alright.

                        MRS. LEWISTON
              Your dad is sick, I'm bringing him
              somewhere to get better.

                        TOM
              That's good.

                        MRS. LEWISTON
              You kind of sad what's wrong, are
              you worried about your dad?

                        TOM
              Well yeah but also have some news
              you won't like, report cards came.

                        MRS. LEWISTON
              Why would I not like that, couldn't
              be that bad.

                        TOM
              I failed two classes.

                    MRS. LEWISTON
          Ah Tom, which classes.

                    TOM
          Science

                    MRS. LEWISTON
          And? What's the other one?

                    TOM
          Math.

                    MRS. LEWISTON
          Tom! How did you fail math, I
          thought you were staying after
          class if you got stuck.

                    TOM
          It's not my fault.

                    MRS. LEWISTON
          How is it not your fault did you
          stay after or not.

                    TOM
          She never stayed behind, she always
          had a meeting or something.

                    MRS. LEWISTON
          I'm sure if you had asked like you
          said you were doing she would have
          helped you.

                    TOM
          I did, she just ignored me, she
          doesn't like me.

                    MRS. LEWISTON
          Don't do this to me Tom, not now.

                    TOM
          Do what?

                    MRS. LEWISTON
          This blaming the teacher thing, I
          can't do it with you again I have
          enough to deal with with your
          father.

                    TOM
          But I did ask, she never stayed.

                         MRS. LEWISTON
               Why would she tell you she will
               stay if she did not stay.

                         TOM
               I don't know. Wait, you don't
               believe me do you?

                         MRS. LEWISTON
               No I don't because it makes no
               sense.

                         TOM
               It is the truth.

                         MRS. LEWISTON
               It is time for you to take
               responsibilities for your actions.

                         TOM
               I can't believe it, you are against
               me just like everyone else.

                         MRS. LEWISTON
               No one is against you Tom, It is
               time for you to grow up!

                         TOM
               You never believe anything I say!

                         MRS. LEWISTON
               Don't you raise your voice at me
               mister, you want to be grounded.

                         TOM
               I don't care.

                         MRS. LEWISTON
               Excuse me?

                         TOM
               I HATE YOU!

                         MRS. LEWISTON
               You don't mean that.

                         TOM
               Yes I do I wish Aunt Charlotte was
               my mom and not you.

SPLIT SCREEN- JOHN'S DINING ROOM AND THE CAR

Tom hangs up, slams the phone down and shoves the glass of
milk off the table.

                                             (CONTINUED)

The glass of milk travels through the air in slow motion.

From the car we see head lights come toward the windshield

Mrs. Lewiston attempts to swerve.

The glass gets closer to the wall

the headlights get brighter

The glass collides with the wall and shatters in slow motion.

At the same time the car is slammed into head on.

JUST JOHNS KITCHEN

Tom collapses against the wall, his face in his hands.

Tom walks into the living room to cry on the couch.

Hours pass and red and blue lights come into the driveway followed by a knock on the door.

Tom goes to the corner of the living room to listen in.

                    OFFICER CONNOLLY
          Good evening mam, are you Charlotte
          Brennan?

                    CHARLOTTE
          Yes, is something wrong.

                    OFFICER CONNOLLY
          Mam is your sisters name Julie
          Lewiston.

                    CHARLOTTE
              (Panicked)
          Julie, is she okay.

                    OFFICER CONNOLLY
          I'm sorry to be the one to have to
          tell you this but your sister was
          involved in a fatal car accident
          earlier this evening.

                    CHARLOTTE
          NOOOO!!!! OH GOD!

Tom runs around the corner to see the officer and his aunt on the floor sobbing uncontrollably.

Tom looks at his aunt in disbelief trying to process it.

                                              (CONTINUED)

Charlotte looks at Tom with tears running down her face.

> TOM
> Aunt Charlotte? What happened.

> OFFICER CONNOLLY
> Are you the son?

> TOM
> Yes, where, where's my dad is he
> okay.

> OFFICER CONNOLLY
> No son, I'm afraid he is not.

> CHARLOTTE
> Henry too? How did this happen?

Tom starts to seem unsteady like his legs are jello.

> OFFICER CONNOLLY
> Well it appears they were struck
> head on by a drunk driver.

> TOM
> It's not true! No they can't be
> dead.

Tom starts to fall and falls right next to his aunt.

Charlotte hugs him tight

Tom breaks into crying.

> OFFICER CONNOLLY
> I can not begin to imagine the pain
> you are feeling right now, I know a
> good grief counselor who does a
> really good job with children.
> Would you like his card.

Charlotte with her hand shaking takes the card

Officer Connolly leaves the house.

INT DR. HARRIS OFFICE DAY

Tom sits uncomfortably looking around the office.

Dr. Harris comes walking in and sits at his desk.

(CONTINUED)

                         DR. HARRIS
                    Well hello Tom, how are we doing
                    today?

Tom just slumps in his seat and looks at the floor remaining
silent.

                         DR. HARRIS
                    Do you want to talk about anything?
                    This is a safe place.

Tom shakes his head.

                         DR. HARRIS
                    Alright, I won't pressure you to
                    say a word. I know you're still
                    hurting Tom, it doesn't go away
                    easily but I am here when you are
                    ready. Your Aunt loves you a lot
                    and she's worried about you.

Tom remains silent.

Dr. Harris takes off his glasses and notepad.

                         DR. HARRIS
                    Tom are you worried about the
                    funeral?

Tom just nods slightly.

                         DR. HARRIS
                    Do you want to stop for the day?

Tom nods.

                         DR. HARRIS
                    Alright we can stop.

Tom B-lines it for the door.

Charlotte meets him in the waiting room.

                         CHARLOTTE
                    Hey that was fast, just wait right
                    here I want to ask the doctor
                    something then we'll go.

Charlotte walks to the door where Dr. Harris is waiting.

                         CHARLOTTE
                    Did he say anything?

                    DR. HARRIS
          I'm afraid not.

                    CHARLOTTE
          Should I be worried, it's been
          three weeks.

                    DR. HARRIS
          Trauma like what Tom went through
          can linger for a long time, I
          believe he will open up in his own
          time, He indicated He was nervous
          about the funeral.

                    CHARLOTTE
          Would medication help?

                    DR. HARRIS
          I don't believe at this time
          medication would be helpful.

                    CHARLOTTE
          Thank you for your help doctor, I
          appreciate it.

                    DR. HARRIS
          You're very welcome, We'll talk
          soon.

                    CHARLOTTE
          Have a good day.

Charlotte walks out of the office with Tom.

INT CHURCH DAY

People file in wearing black

Piano plays funeral music

                    PRIEST
          Good morning all, on this day of
          tragedy i would like to read a
          passage from the book of wisdom,
          Chapter 3 verse 1-3.

People bow their heads.

                    PRIEST
           The souls of the righteous are in
          the hand of god, and no torment
          shall touch them. They seemed in
                    (MORE)

                         PRIEST (cont'd)
                    the view of the foolish; to be
                    dead,

Tom raises his head toward the two caskets and begins to
walk up to them tears in his eyes.

                         PRIEST
                    And their passing away was thought
                    to be an affliction, and their
                    going forth from us, utter
                    destruction, but they are in peace.
                    AMEN

The church looks at Tom

Tom kneels before his parents caskets and cries

Charlotte walks up to him to comfort him puts her hands on
his shoulders.

Tom speaks for the first time in 4 weeks.

                         TOM
                    I'm sorry mom, I'm sorry dad. It's
                    all my fault.

                         CHARLOTTE
                    It's all going to be alright Tom

Tom cries harder and Charlotte hugs him tight.

INT DR. HARRIS OFFICE DAY

5 years later.

Tom walks into the office now a high school student and sits
in his seat with headphones in.

Dr. Harris comes in the room talking but Tom doesn't hear
him.

Dr. Harris taps Tom on the shoulder

Tom jumps and takes his headphones off.

                         DR. HARRIS
                    A little jumpy today?

Tom laughs and puts his headphones down around his neck

                    TOM
          I'm sorry Dr. H I didn't hear you.

                    DR. HARRIS
          How are you doing today Tom

                    TOM
          Feeling pretty decent, I went for a
          drive.

                    DR. HARRIS
          Where did you go.

                    TOM
          I know what you're going to say but
          I had to see to go back.

                    DR. HARRIS
          Back where Tom?

                    TOM
          I drove past my old house, I
          haven't been there since the night
          my parents died.

                    DR. HARRIS
          I see, and?

                    TOM
          It looks so different.

                    DR. HARRIS
          Different how?

EXT TOMS OLD HOUSE DAY

Tom drives up in his car and stops in front of the house and
puts the car in park but keeps the engine on.

                    TOM
          It looks abandoned, all the grass
          is overgrown and there are broken
          windows.

Tom shakes his head in disbelieve, puts the car in drive and
drives away.

INT DR. HARRIS OFFICE DAY

Dr. harris is taking notes on what Tom is saying.

              TOM
        It wasn't my home, it was so empty
        and lifeless, just a shell of
        something that once existed.

              DR. HARRIS
        Have you ever considered being a
        writer?

Tom looks confused.

              TOM
        Never really thought about it

              DR. HARRIS
        The way you speak, I think you
        could be a good writer especially
        for poetry and it might help
        release some anxiousness.

Dr. Harris reaches in his desk and pulls out a empty journal
and gives it to Tom.

              DR. HARRIS
        I want you to write in this when
        you can, just what you're feeling,
        how the day was, anything you want.

EXT CEMETERY DAY

Tom pulls up in his car and gets out with flowers in his
hand.

Tom puts flowers on his mothers grave and kneels beside it
with his head down in silence for a moment.

              TOM
        I miss you guys so much. Everyone
        says the pain will dull with time
        but I doubt that.

Tom sits in front of the two graves.

              TOM
        I still dream about that night like
        it was yesterday, I wish I could go
        back, I wish I could feel your hugs
        again mom. I

(CONTINUED)

Tom wipes his eyes as they are watering.

>   TOM
>   I wish you were here, High school
>   has been so hard without you two. I
>   constantly get picked on, and i
>   still have one more year to go.

Tom bows his head.

>   TOM
>   Please send me the strength to get
>   through this last year, I feel so
>   lost.

Another car pulls to the cemetery

Tom kisses his mothers grave stone and his fathers and
stands up.

Tom puts the flowers down at his mothers grave.

>   TOM
>   I'll see ya.

Tom leaves the cemetery.

EXT SCHOOL PARKING LOT MORNING

Tom and John standing by their car before the school day
starts.

>   JOHN
>   It will all be different this year
>   Tom you'll see we're seniors now.

>   TOM
>   The only thing I'm looking forward
>   to is graduating from this shit
>   hole.

>   JOHN
>   It shouldn't be too bad, at least
>   we have Science together.

>   TOM
>   Yeah that's true I guess.

>   JOHN
>   You alright man?

                              TOM
               I visited my old house yesterday
               and went to my parents grave after
               the appointment with Dr. Harris, I
               still miss them man.

                              JOHN
               I'm sorry Tom, what did Dr. Harris
               say?

                              TOM
               To write in this journal all of my
               feelings. He says I should think
               about being a writer. Like I'm
               going to pour my thoughts on a page
               like a Edgar Allen Poe or
               something. "quote the raven
               nevermore."

                              JOHN
               Well you always got me to talk to
               brother.

                              TOM
               I know man, It's nothing really
               just not sleeping lately.

                              JOHN
               We should get in there man, what do
               you have first?

                              TOM
               Yeah I suppose you're right, I have
               English.

                              JOHN
               Lucky, I'm stuck with Math.

Tom and John start heading for the school.

                              JOHN
               Hey man good luck, I'll see you at
               break.

                              TOM
               Yeah see ya.

INT CLASSROOM DAY

Kids file into the classroom

Tom sits in the back of the room.

The teacher is writing on the board "who I am"

Tom looks around at his classmates and sees Glen.

                    TOM
          You have to be kidding me.

Tom puts his head down

The bell rings.

Tom falls asleep for almost the whole class.

                    MRS. WINTERS
          Alright class have a seat.

Mrs. Winters points to the board.

                    MRS. WINTERS
          Our first assignment, we'll go
          around the room and I want you to
          all answer this question. Lets
          start with you.

Mrs. Winters points to Tom.

Tom wakes up and sees she is pointing at him.

                    TOM
          Me?

                    MRS. WINTERS
          Yes, share a little about yourself.

                    TOM
          I'd rather not, I'm not that
          interesting.

                    MRS. WINTERS
          Come on, Don't be shy just a little
          something.

Tom stands up and looks around the room.

                    TOM
          Alright, I guess hi my name is Tom.

Glen throws a big paper ball at him.

(CONTINUED)

The class starts to laugh.

                    TOM
          Do I have to do this?

                    MRS. WINTERS
          What do you like to do?

                    TOM
          I don't know, play hacky sack.

                    MRS. WINTERS
          Anything else? What do you when you
          and your friends aren't in school.

                    GLEN
          What friends? He's a loser.

                    MRS. WINTERS
          Glen first warning.

                    TOM
          I have friends.

Glen scoffs (makes pffft sound)

                    GLEN
          You mean your no good cousin the
          ginger.

Tom turns to Glen and opens his mouth to yell.

Kurtis interrupts him.

                    KURTIS
          Ah shut up Glen.

                    GLEN
          What did you say to me.

Kurtis stands up.

                    KURTIS
          Shouldn't you have graduated by
          now? what are you a 2nd year
          senior?

                    GLEN
          It was a mistake with the school.

                    KURTIS
          Right, it's the schools fault
          you're fat and slow.

The other kids laugh.

>   MRS. WINTERS
>   Who are you?

>   KURTIS
>   That is the assignment isn't it, Hi
>   my name is Kurtis and the one thing
>   to know about me is I hate bullies
>   like him. Picking on younger kids,
>   your parents must be really proud
>   Glen.

Glen looks at Tom.

>   GLEN
>   Yeah, they are and at least I have
>   parents.

Tom stands up flips and flips his desk.

>   KURTIS
>   whoa easy, porky pig isn't worth
>   it.

The class laughs.

>   GLEN
>   Make fun of me and see what happens
>   punk.

>   KURTIS
>   It sucks when the class is laughing
>   at you doesn't it, I'm not afraid
>   of you pal.

Mrs. Winters gets on the phone to the office.

Glen stands up.

The bell rings.

>   GLEN
>   This isn't over Tom, I'll get you
>   both for this.

Glen walks out of the class.

Kurtis helps Tom put his desk back.

>   TOM
>   Thanks for that.

                         KURTIS
              No problem, I'm Kurtis.

Tom shakes his hand.

                         TOM
              Yeah, I guessed that, I'm Tom.

                         KURTIS
              You don't remember me do you?

                         TOM
              Should I?

                         KURTIS
              Nah man, I expect not. Off to the
              office, have a good one.

                         TOM
              Yeah, same to you.

Tom stands there confused for a minute not used to people
talking to him and sticking up for him.

He puts on his bag and walks to the door

Tom stops and turns to Mrs. Winters.

                         TOM
              Sorry about the desk Mrs. winters.

INT CAFETERIA DAY

Tom and John are siting at a table during break between
classes.

                         JOHN
              And he just stood up to Glen?

                         TOM
              I'm telling you man it was awesome.
              I wish I could have punched Glen.

Kurtis comes walking to the cafeteria

                         TOM
              Hey here he is now.

Tom waves to get Kurtis's attention.

Kurtis walks over to the table and sits.

                         KURTIS
          Hey guys.

                         TOM
          Hey, this is John.

                         KURTIS
          What's going on I'm Kurtis.

                         JOHN
          Tom was telling me about English
          class, did you really stand up to
          Glen?

                         KURTIS
          Yeah, He's all talk, He won't do
          anything.

                         JOHN
          That is great I wish I could have
          been there to see that.

                         TOM
          Glen has been picking on us for
          years and no one has put him in his
          place like that.

                         KURTIS
          Well hopefully now he'll knock it
          off. Do you mind if my girlfriend
          sits here and we hang out with you
          guys?

                         JOHN
          You want to hang out with us?

                         KURTIS
          Yeah, why not.

                         TOM
          Well it just never happens, usually
          people just ignore us.

                         KURTIS
          Well I'll chill here.

                         JOHN
          So who's your girlfriend.

Katie comes walking in, dressed in her cheerleader uniform
chatting with people in the hall as she enters.

                              JOHN
               Wow, Katie Caron, What a bombshell.

Katie turns and starts walking to the table.

                              JOHN
               Holy crap is she walking over here?

                              KURTIS
               Well I sure hope she is.

Katie comes up to the table and stands with Kurtis.

John is wide eyed and speechless.

                              KURTIS
               Hey babe.

                              KATIE
               Hey there, who's your new friends.

Katie turns to Tom.

Tom reaches out his hand.

                              KURTIS
               This is Tom.

                              TOM
               Hi.

Katie turns to John and shakes his hand.

                              JOHN
               Hello I'm John

                              KATIE
               Good to meet you guys.

                              TOM
               It is?

                              KATIE
               Yeah, you seem surprised.

                              TOM
               I am a little.

                              KATIE
               Why's that, because I'm a
               cheerleader?

                         TOM
          Well yeah, Kinda.

                         KURTIS
          Uh oh now ya did it.

                         TOM
          What did I say?

                         KURTIS
          Katie doesn't like being labeled
          with them.

                         KATIE
          That's right, it's not like we're
          all stuck up rich snob bullies. I
          go and cheer because it's what I
          like to do, I don't fit in with
          them.

Katie waves to the cheerleaders and they sarcastically wave
back and whisper together laughing.

                         KATIE
          See, I'm not one of them, I never
          will be.

Tom puts his hands up.

                         TOM
          Alright, My bad. She's passionate
          I'll give you that.

                         KURTIS
          Oh you have no idea

Kurtis winks at Tom

Katie elbows Tom

They all laugh.

                         JOHN
          So how did you guys meet.

Katie Smiles.

                         KURTIS
          That would be 2 years ago at
          Homecoming, I had some game let me
          tell ya.

                                KATIE
                    Yeah, is that what you call it.

                                KURTIS
                    Haha, alright here's what really
                    happened.

INT HIGH SCHOOL GYM NIGHT

Kurtis is bobbing his head to the music and drinking a cup
of punch.

                                KURTIS
                            (to himself)
                    Alright, Tonight is definitely the
                    night. You can do it man.

Kids walk by the punch bowl and Kurtis stops talking to
himself and just does the head nod.

                                KURTIS
                            (to himself)
                    Just walk up to a girl and talk to
                    her. Now we just have to find one.

Kurtis looks around the room and sees a girl alone and
starts to walk over.

A guy walks up to her and hugs her.

Kurtis steps back to the punch bowl just scanning the dance.

the crowd parts a little and Katie comes through the crowd
toward the punch bowl.

                                KURTIS
                            (To himself)
                    Wow.

Kurtis takes a huge breath and sips his drink nervously

Katie walks up and gets a drink

                                KURTIS
                    Hi.

                                KATIE
                    Hello

Kurtis doesn't make eye contact and they stand their
awkwardly.

Kurtis looks at her and goes to speak but doesn't.

                                                    (CONTINUED)

                              KURTIS
                    Mm this is good punch huh?

                              KATIE
                    What? oh yeah, It's pretty good I
                    guess.

Kurtis turns his head away from her and mumbles to himself.

Katie looks at him shyly.

Kurtis turns to her.

                              KURTIS
                    Awesome dance, cheers.

Kurtis waves his drink in a cheer motion and then takes a
sip but spills a bunch on his shirt.

Kurtis goes to wipe it up really quick.

Katie looks at him and cracks a smile.

                              KURTIS
                    I'm messing this up.

                              KATIE
                    Messing up what?

Katie and Kurtis look at each other smiling for a minute.

                              KURTIS
                    Would you like to?

                              KATIE
                    Would I like to what?

                              KURTIS
                    You know, dance with me?

                              KATIE
                    I'd love to.

                              KURTIS
                    I understand if you don't, wait you
                    just said yes.

Katie laughs and nods.

Kurtis smiles and holds out his hand.

Katie takes his hand and they walk to the dance floor.

Stairway to heaven plays and they dance looking into each other eyes.

Katie hugs Kurtis as the song goes on.

INT CAFETERIA DAY

Katie is smiling and hugs Kurtis.

>   KURTIS
>   And once I had her looking, she
>   couldn't resist my charm.

>   KATIE
>   What charm is that now?

>   KURTIS
>   Oh you know the charm, all I have
>   to do is smile and you do what I
>   want.

>   KATIE
>   Excuse me? That's me thank you.

>   KURTIS
>   Damn I always get those mixed up.

Katie and Kurtis laugh and kiss.

>   JOHN
>   Wow man, I wish I had your
>   confidence.

>   KURTIS
>   I may be confident now but I was
>   scared then.

>   KATIE
>   It's true.

Frank comes in knocking over a trashcan and freaking out.

Kids laugh at him

Kurtis, Katie, Tom, John all turn around.

>   TOM
>   Who's that.

>   KURTIS
>   His name is Frank.

                         JOHN
          Why is he freaking out like that?

                         KATIE
          Well rumor is he is a schizto,
          Hears voices.

                         KATIE
          It's sad really.

The bell rings and everyone gets there bags and starts to
work to the next class.

Kurtis kisses Katie.

                         KURTIS
          See you when I see you guys, and
          Tom don't worry about Glen he's all
          talk and I have your back.

                         TOM
          Thanks man. Nice to meet you Katie

                         KATIE
          Yeah nice to meet you too, see you
          guys around.

Everyone gets their bag on and heads out the door.

INT CLASSROOM DAY

Kids pile into the classroom.

Mr. Platsberg comes walking in unenthusiastically

Jack comes in and shyly sits down.

A group of kids sit near Jack snickering.

Kurtis sits near Tom.

                         MR. PLATSBERG
          Alright welcome to Environmental
          science please take a seat.

                         KURTIS
          Hey Tom.

                         TOM
          Hey man, you're in this class too.

                          KURTIS
               Yeah, unfortunately needed a
               science credit to graduate.

                          TOM
               Is this class hard?

                          KURTIS
               Nah, it's more boring than hard.

                          MR. PLATSBERG
               Alright I'm going to have you just
               read chapter 1 on your own on the
               layers of the earth and we'll
               discuss it, or something.

Mr. Platsberg draws a visual of the layers and lines to be
labeled and sits at his desk.

Jack is working quietly when he is hit by a spitball.

Jack ignores the first one and continues reading.

Jack is hit again and looks up and over.

two jocks are laughing at him.

                          JACK
               Stop, I'm trying to read.

Kurtis looks over and sees the kids snickering.

Mr. Platsberg sits at his desk.

The jocks throw paper balls at Jack.

                          JACK
               I said Leave me alone.

                          MR. PLATSBERG
               Jack please be quiet, there are
               people trying to read and learn in
               here.

                          JACK
               Yeah, but they won't leave me
               alone. They keep chucking things at
               me.

                          MR. PLATSBERG
               All I see right now is you
               interrupting my class.

                        KURTIS
          Well maybe you should pay more
          attention then.

The class snickers.

                        MR. PLATSBERG
          Did you say something?

                        KURTIS
          Hm, you missed that one too did ya,
          not very observant.

The class laughs.

                        MR. PLATSBERG
          Is there a problem?

                        KURTIS
          Yes there is, you don't care about
          your job so you're not doing it,
          whether it's because you've been in
          here too long or they are not
          paying you enough but you are not
          doing your job, a job we as some of
          us actually help pay for.

                        MR. PLATSBERG
          I do my job.

Kurtis laughs.

                        KURTIS
          Really? you're job is to yell at
          kids when they are being picked on?

                        MR. PLATSBERG
          I don't get paid to hold hands.

                        KURTIS
          No it sure looks like your job is
          to sit there with a sour look and a
          thumb up your ass.

Kurtis stands up and gets his backpack on.

Kurtis starts to walk toward the door.

                        MR. PLATSBERG
          Hey, where do you think you are
          going I'm not done with you yet.

>   KURTIS
>   Yeah? well I'm done with you, and
>   for my two cents before I go. If
>   you don't like your job, just
>   fucking retire.

Kurtis leaves the room.

The class cheers him on.

Tom shakes his head laughing.

Even Jack cracks a smile.

Mr. Platsberg just sits down.

>   MR. PLATSBERG
>   Alright everyone show is over back
>   to your books.

EXT HIGH SCHOOL PARKING LOT AFTERNOON

John and Tom exit the school and start walking towards Tom's
car and stops.

Glen grins from the passenger side of the car and points to
them.

>   TOM
>   Great, now we get to deal with him.

>   JOHN
>   Maybe He's over what happened in
>   class.

Glen starts letting air out of the tires.

>   TOM
>   Yeah?

>   JOHN
>   Well wishful thinking I guess.

A car horn honks.

Tom and John turn.

Kurtis waves them over.

>   KURTIS
>   Hey you guys want a ride.

                         TOM
               Yeah definitely.

                         JOHN
               Great timing dude.

John and Tom sit in the back seat

                         KURTIS
               Hey guys, we just have to drop
               Katie off first.

                         JOHN
               Hey Katie.

                         KATIE
               Hi John.

Kurtis Drives off from the parking lot.

INT CAR DAY

Katie sits up front quiet

John and Tom sit awkwardly in the back.

                         KURTIS
               So how was the rest of science
               class after I left?

                         TOM
               Well your speech was definitely the
               highlight, all he did was sit at
               his desk and the class pretended to
               read their books.

                         KATIE
               Speech?

                         KURTIS
               It's nothing really, just some
               bullies in the class and a lazy
               teacher.

Katie sighs

                         KURTIS
               What?

Katie rolls her eyes and looks out the window.

                                              (CONTINUED)

                              KURTIS
                    Are you giving me the silent
                    treatment?

Katie doesn't answer him.

                              KURTIS
                    Hm, fantastic. I'm the bad guy

Tom and John sit in the back silent feeling a little
awkward.

Moments later Katie turns her head to look at Kurtis.

                              KATIE
                    You know they could suspend you if
                    you're not careful.

                              KURTIS
                    Come on don't be dramatic they
                    won't suspend me, we go to the
                    school that takes no action.

                              KATIE
                    I just want to see you graduate,
                    why do you feel the need to fight
                    every battle.

                              KURTIS
                    I do it because no one else will,
                    because I've been that victim. I do
                    it for her.

                              KATIE
                    Okay.

Kurtis pulls up to Katie's house.

                              KURTIS
                    What's with you today? You've been
                    acting really spacey.

                              KATIE
                    It's nothing just forget it.

Kurtis puts the car in park and turns to Katie.

Kurtis reaches for Katie's hand

Katie grabs her bag and gets out of the car.

Kurtis drops his head and groans.

                    KURTIS
          Guys I'll be right back, I have to
          go figure out this out.

Kurtis leaves the car and runs to Katie.

Tom and John look at each other shocked and a little
confused.

Katie and Kurtis are having a heated emotional conversation
in the background but you can't hear them.

                    TOM
          Wow, what was that about do you
          think.

                    JOHN
          I don't know and who is her?

                    TOM
          Who knows, a ex maybe.

                    JOHN
          Here he comes.

Kurtis walks back and gets in the car.

Kurtis puts the car in drive and starts driving down the
road.

                    KURTIS
          Sorry about that guys.

                    TOM
          What happened?

                    KURTIS
          I don't know she's been acting
          really strange, getting sick and
          moody.

                    JOHN
          Who were you talking about when you
          said her?

                    KURTIS
          What?

                    JOHN
          You said you do it for her.

                         KURTIS
               Really not worth getting into right
               now man.

                         JOHN
               Alright sorry.

                         KURTIS
               It's all good.

                         TOM
               This is it right here.

Kurtis pulls up to Johns house and drops them off.

                         TOM
               Hey thanks for the ride, do you
               wanna hang out? we're going to play
               some hacky sack.

                         KURTIS
               Nah, not today man maybe next week.

                         TOM
               Alright man that's cool, well see
               you in school.

Kurtis rolls up his window and drives away.

INT JOHN'S KITCHEN NIGHT

Tom walks into the fridge to grab a soda.

Charlotte is arguing on the phone with someone

Tom grabs cracks the soda open and sips it.

                         JOHN
               Hey can you grab me a soda too
               while you're in there?

                         TOM
               Yeah sure.

                         CHARLOTTE
               Are you serious? What kind of
               school are you running over there.

Charlotte is pacing in the kitchen while water is boiling.

Tom Grabs another soda and reaches in the cabinet for
Doritos.

(CONTINUED)

Charlotte covers the phone.

                    CHARLOTTE
          Hey, Ah, don't eat a bunch of stuff
          dinner will be ready soon.

Tom nods and eats a few chips and puts them back.

Tom walks out of the kitchen.

INT JOHN'S DINING ROOM NIGHT

Tom hands John his soda.

John cracks it open.

John is working on math homework.

Tom has his history book out.

                    CHARLOTTE
          All those teachers around and no
          one saw a thing? You really want me
          to believe that?

                    TOM
          Wow, your mom is really ripping
          into the principal.

                    JOHN
          Yeah, she was pretty pissed about
          the car.

                    CHARLOTTE
          Well thank you very much for
          nothing.

Charlotte walks into the dining room with a stack of mail
and frustrated.

                    CHARLOTTE
          That man is absolutely ridiculous,
          telling me there were no witnesses.
          Maybe if he didn't have his head up
          his ass.

John looks up from his book at his mom.

                    CHARLOTTE
          You saw Glen letting the air out of
          the tires?

                                        (CONTINUED)

                        TOM
          Yes, but I doubt the school will do
          anything.

                        CHARLOTTE
          Why?

                        TOM
          His dad is on the board and really
          good friends with the principal.

                        CHARLOTTE
          well we can't afford a tow right
          now so do you have another way to
          school, I'm sure you don't want to
          take a bus.

                        TOM
          Yeah, I think we can talk to
          Kurtis.

Charlotte starts looking through the mail at the bills and
sighs in frustration.

                        JOHN
          Are you alright mom.

                        CHARLOTTE
          It just never stops coming, these
          bills are piling up.

                        TOM
          It will be alright Aunt Charlotte.

Tom puts his arm around Charlotte's shoulder.

                        TOM
          Too bad that piece of shit couldn't
          have stuck around and been the
          father He should have been.

                        CHARLOTTE
          Don't say that about him, He was a
          good man.

                        TOM
          If He was He would be here, why are
          you defending him?

                        CHARLOTTE
          I just don't want to talk about it,
          you don't know the whole story.

                                          (CONTINUED)

                         JOHN
          I think Tom's right mom.

                         CHARLOTTE
          John, just drop it.

                         JOHN
          Alright jeez.

Charlotte grabs her head in pain.

                         CHARLOTTE
          I'm sorry, I just wish for once,
          just once we could get a little
          good news. Tom can you go put these
          papers in my dresser.

                         TOM
          Sure.

Tom grabs the papers and heads down the hall.

INT. CHARLOTTE'S ROOM NIGHT

Tom walks into the room and heads to the dresser with the
papers.

Tom opens the drawer and puts the papers in.

Tom goes to shut the dresser but A picture catches his eye
of his mom and dad and him as a baby.

Tom stares at the photo and smiles and his lip begins to
quiver like he's about to sob.

Tom sniffles and goes to put the the picture back but grabs
another piece of paper that was under the picture.

Tom realizes that it's John's birth certificate and as he
reads on a Look of intense shock and confusion slowly
appears.

Toms eyes widen in horror and his breathing becomes labored.

Tom puts the document back where he got it and slowly
stumbles back to the dining room.

INT JOHN'S DINING ROOM NIGHT

John is taking notes and Charlotte is drinking a glass of
wine.

> CHARLOTTE
> Dinner is ready guys if you want
> it.

> TOM
> What.

Tom is still dazed and sits down at the table

> CHARLOTTE
> Are you feeling alright Tom?

> TOM
> No, actually I'm feeling really
> sick at the moment.

> CHARLOTTE
> Well let me get you a plate.

Charlotte puts her glass down and walks away.

> JOHN
> Dude are you alright?

> TOM
> No, I am not.

> JOHN
> What's up?

> TOM
> I can't really think straight right
> now.

Tom takes deep breathes

Charlotte comes back in with a plate of Nuggets.

Tom takes the nuggets and eats one.

> CHARLOTTE
> Is that helping?

> TOM
> Please don't talk to me right now.

                         CHARLOTTE
          What?

                         TOM
          I can't believe you would do that.

                         CHARLOTTE
          Do what? What are you talking about
          Tom?

                         TOM
          I'm not hungry, and Lets just say I
          know the whole story now.

Tom slides the plate across the table and runs off down the
hall to his room.

Charlotte stands there confused and then realizes what Tom
is talking about.

Charlotte covers her mouth.

                         CHARLOTTE
          Oh no.

                         JOHN
          What's wrong with him?

                         CHARLOTTE
          Nothing, just eat your supper and
          I'll go talk to him.

Charlotte walks off down the hall.

John sits there confused.

TOM/JOHN'S ROOM NIGHT

Charlotte walks in and taps on the door.

Tom wipes away some tears and doesn't turn to face her.

                         TOM
          Go away.

                         CHARLOTTE
          Tom listen to me we have to talk
          about this.

                         TOM
          Why? so you can lie a little more.

                              CHARLOTTE
                    I know you're angry at me, you have
                    every right to be but you can't
                    tell him what you saw.

                              TOM
                    He has a right to know you betrayed
                    him.

                              CHARLOTTE
                    I tried so hard to tell him and I
                    will tell him, just let him here it
                    from me please.

                              TOM
                    How can you ask me to keep such a
                    big secret?

                              CHARLOTTE
                    I know it's asking a lot.

                              TOM
                    I can't make any promises, now just
                    leave me alone I need to think.

                              CHARLOTTE
                    Alright, goodnight.

Charlotte turns to walk out but stops.

Charlotte looks down.

                              CHARLOTTE
                    I love you Tom. I hope you know
                    that.

Tom doesn't look up or say anything.

Charlotte walks away.

Tom lays down.

The night flashes by and the sun comes up, Tom doesn't sleep
a wink. The days seem to blur and a week has already passed.

INT DR. HARRIS OFFICE DAY

A weary and Exhausted Tom sits slumped in the chair, Bags
under his eyes yawning.

Dr. Harris Looks at Tom with concern.

                              TOM
                    You know I don't like it when you
                    stare at me like that.

                              DR. HARRIS
                    Can I get you anything to drink?

                              TOM
                    Do you have coffee? Can't seem to
                    wake up.

                              DR. HARRIS
                    Sure, Cream? Sugar?

                              TOM
                    Just black please.

Dr. Harris walks over to a coffee pot in his office and
pours Tom a cup of coffee.

Dr. Harris hands Tom the coffee

Tom takes it and smells it.

Tom smiles and sips at it.

                              TOM
                    Thank you Doc.

                              DR. HARRIS
                    You're very welcome Tom.

Tom rubs his eyes and stretches his arm.

Tom notices the calendar.

                              TOM
                    What day is it?

                              DR. HARRIS
                    It's Tuesday.

                              TOM
                    The days have been blurring
                    together the last week, I haven't
                    slept much.

                              DR. HARRIS
                    Is everything alright at home?

                              TOM
                    No, not really.

                                                    (CONTINUED)

                    DR. HARRIS
          What's going on?

                    TOM
          I have information that I stumbled
          upon recently that changes how I
          see my aunt.

                    DR. HARRIS
          What kind of information?

                    TOM
          I don't want to say but the kind
          that makes me feel betrayed, a lie
          that's been hidden all these years,
          and she wants me to not tell John.

                    DR. HARRIS
          Why would she not want you to tell
          him?

                    TOM
          It involves him, and she betrayed
          him, he deserves to know though.

                    DR. HARRIS
          Well how will he react?

                    TOM
          It's going to upset him for sure.

                    DR. HARRIS
          Is that why you aren't sleeping
          well.

                    TOM
          I had a dream and it seemed like a
          message.

                    DR. HARRIS
          is it the same dream you couldn't
          remember?

                    TOM
          Yeah.

                    DR. HARRIS
          Tell me about the dream.

                    TOM
          Alright it starts on the beach.

EXT BEACH DAY

Kids are splashing in the water and playing on the
playground.

Tom smiles and sits on a bench just looking at the water.

                    TOM
                 (Voice over)
          I sit, and I can feel the warmth of
          the sun, it's calming.

                    DR. HARRIS
                 (Voice Over)
          Then what happens.

Tom looks over and sees his mom helping him build a
sandcastle as a young kid. They are laughing and having a
lot of fun.

                    TOM
                 (voice over)
          I see her.

                    DR. HARRIS
                 (Voice over)
          You see who?

                    TOM
                 (Voice over)
          My mother, we were building
          sandcastles together.

Tom smiles

                    TOM
                 (voice over)
          I called to her, but.

Tom tries to speak but no sound comes out.

                    DR. HARRIS
          But what?

                    TOM
          No sound came out of my mouth.

                    DR. HARRIS
          So what did you do.

Tom starts to walk toward his mother and his younger self.

(CONTINUED)

                              TOM
                    I am so happy and all I want to do
                    is reach her and then something
                    happens.

                         DR. HARRIS
                    What happens Tom.

The wind starts to pick up and the sky darkens.

                              TOM
                    All the sudden it gets dark and
                    windy, and then I hear a loud pop.

                         DR. HARRIS
                    Thunder?

                              TOM
                    No, sounds more like a gunshot and
                    I turn.

Tom turns to see what the sound is and turns back to find
the beach is empty and his mother gone.

                              TOM
                    And then she's gone and I feel
                    scared.

                         DR. HARRIS
                    What are you scared of Tom.

                              TOM
                    Something bad is coming, it's
                    getting darker.

INT DR. HARRIS OFFICE DAY

Another gunshot rings out and Tom jumps in his chair, nearly
spilling the coffee.

                              TOM
                    And that's when I wake up.

Dr. Harris finishes scribbling in his notes and looks at Tom
taking his glasses off.

                         DR. HARRIS
                    Well, that is some dream.

                              TOM
                    What do you think it means?

                         DR. HARRIS
               Well I think with this big secret
               you're keeping your subconscious is
               pointing out your stress and you
               miss your mother. What do you take
               it as?

                         TOM
               I don't know, I can't shake this
               feeling though.

                         DR. HARRIS
               What feeling is that?

                         TOM
               Something really bad is coming.

Dr. Harris looks at Tom for a moment, then takes his glasses
off and rubs his eyes.

Dr. harris glances at the clock.

                         DR. HARRIS
               Well time's up for today, same time
               next week. For sleep try melatonin
               tonight.

                         TOM
               Alright, what about the secret I
               found out? Should I tell him?

                         DR. HARRIS
               Maybe you should, keeping it in is
               causing you a lot of stress,is it a
               major shock?

                         TOM
               I don't want to get into it but
               thank you for the advice doc.

                         DR. HARRIS
               My door is always open and you can
               call too.

                         TOM
               Alright, have a good one.

Tom begins to leave.

                         DR. HARRIS
               Oh hey Tom, you didn't bring your
               journal.

                         TOM
               Yeah, I'm still writing in it but
               I'll get it to you next week.

                         DR. HARRIS
               Fair enough, get some sleep.

                         TOM
               I'll try.

Tom leaves the office.

INT TOM'S CAR DAY

Tom gets in the car where John is waiting.

                         JOHN
               There you are, how did it go.

                         TOM
               Like it always does, I told him I
               wasn't sleeping and He recommended
               a sleep aid called Melatonin.

                         JOHN
               Will it help?

                         TOM
               He said it should so we're going to
               run to the pharmacy on the way home
               and pick some up.

                         JOHN
               Cool, so what's up with you and my
               mom man?

                         TOM
               What do you mean?

                         JOHN
               Well it just seems like you guys
               aren't getting along lately, like
               there is some tension.

                         TOM
               Well what did she say?

                         JOHN
               She told me it is just you getting
               frustrated about school and missing
               your parents.

Tom starts the car.

                         TOM
              Your mom is right about one thing,
              I do miss my parents every but that
              is not why I freaked out last week.

                         JOHN
              So why did you freak out?

Tom puts on his seat belt and puts the car in drive.

Tom takes a deep breath and looks at John.

                         TOM
              I, I just know.. things now that
              change everything.

                         JOHN
              What things?

Tom draws a frustrated breath and starts to drive away.

                         TOM
              Just things that you should know,
              and that I don't want to talk about
              right now, we will talk later.

INT PHARMACY DAY

Tom and John are walking up and down the pharmacy aisles
looking at different products trying to find the sleep aids.

                         JOHN
              What's it called again?

                         TOM
              Melatonin.

John points at the sign above the aisle.

                         JOHN
              Well its says that aisle is
              sleep-aids and pain relievers.

Tom and John walk to the aisle over and start looking
through the Items.

                         TOM
              I found Tylenol PM and Advil PM so
              we have to be getting close.

                    JOHN
               Hey I found it right here
               Melatonin.

John picks up the bottle and shows it to Tom.

                    TOM
               Yup, that's the one.

John tosses the bottle to Tom.

Tom catches the bottle.

                    JOHN
               So is that all we had to get?

                    TOM
               Yeah, but do you want a Dew or
               something?

                    JOHN
               Yeah sure I could go for a Pepsi
               actually.

                    TOM
               And perhaps some slim Jim action.

                    JOHN
               Hell yeah man let's do it up.

John and Tom high five each other and walk toward the
fridge.

                    JOHN
               So that ride home from Kurtis was
               pretty awkward huh?

                    TOM
               Yeah for sure, she was pissed at
               him for something.

                    JOHN
               I wonder what though, you don't
               think Kurtis cheated on her do you?

                    TOM
               No definitely not He seems better
               than that.

                    JOHN
               Maybe Katie just gets jealous
               really easily, I would love to ask
               her.

                              TOM
                    Well here's your chance.

John looks up

                              JOHN
                    What?

Tom points to Katie at the Pharmacy Counter.

Katie starts walking away not noticing them.

                              JOHN
                    Hey Katie.

Katie turns around with a look of surprise and tries to hide
her purchase.

                              KATIE
                    Hey John, Hey Tom, what are you
                    guys doing here?

                              TOM
                    Just buying something to help me
                    sleep I hope.

                              JOHN
                    What are you up to?

                              KATIE
                    Nothing, who says I'm up to
                    anything?

Katie shields her purchase from view.

                              TOM
                    Why were buying something at the
                    pharmacy? Are you sick?

Katie looks at the bag.

Katie acts nervously

                              KATIE
                    Oh this? It's nothing really just
                    some feminine products, listen I
                    really gotta go I'll see you guys
                    in school.

Katie walks away hastily.

Tom and John exchange puzzled looks.

                              TOM
                    What was that all about?

                              JOHN
                    I don't know, did it seem like she
                    was trying to hide something?

                              TOM
                    Yeah I got that too.

                              JOHN
                    I don't think I'll ever understand
                    women.

                              TOM
                    You are not alone my friend.

Tom and John grab their Mountain Dew and grab the slim-Jims
on the way to the counter.

Tom pays for the pays for everything and they leave.

INT CAFETERIA DAY

Tom and John are sitting around the lunch Table.

Tom struggles to stay awake and has bags under his eyes.

Kurtis comes up and sits down.

                              KURTIS
                    Wow dude you look like shit.

                              TOM
                    Thanks I try.

                              KURTIS
                    Seriously when's the last time you
                    slept?

                              TOM
                    I sleep a couple hours here and
                    there but I haven't really got a
                    good rest in weeks.

                              KURTIS
                    Something bothering you?

                              TOM
                    Yes and no, I have some stuff on my
                    mind but the good thing is at least
                    Glen hasn't bothered me since that
                    day in English.

                        JOHN
          Thanks to you Kurtis.

                        KURTIS
          I knew he was just all talk, that
          revenge thing was BS.

Tom yawns heavily and struggles to keep his eyes open.

                        KURTIS
          Seriously dude maybe you should go
          to the nurse or something.

                        TOM
          Maybe after next period I will.

                        JOHN
          Hey where's Katie?

                        KURTIS
          Oh she's at home she was throwing
          up this morning.

                        TOM
          Things alright between you two?

                        KURTIS
          Yeah I don't know, she's been rough
          around the edges lately.

                        JOHN
          We saw her the other day at the
          pharmacy and she was acting very
          strange.

                        KURTIS
          Really?

                        TOM
          Yeah I think she didn't want us to
          know what she bought or something.

                        KURTIS
          Strange, yeah she's been acting
          weird and getting sick a lot
          lately.

Glen comes into the cafeteria and over to the table.

                        GLEN
          Hey it's the Three Stooges, What's
          up guys.

Kurtis stands up.

                         GLEN
          Oh, the tough guy of the group.

                         TOM
          What do you want Glen?

                         GLEN
          I can't just stop by and see my
          friends?

                         JOHN
          We're not your friends.

                         TOM
          Yeah you're just the asshole shit
          all the time.

                         GLEN
          Wow that hurts, I even left you a
          present in your locker to show how
          much I want to be friends.

                         KURTIS
          I think you should leave.

                         GLEN
          Alright alright I'm going.

Glen gets up and starts walking towards the door.

                         TOM
          What do you mean present?

                         GLEN
          Oh you'll see.

Glen walks away laughing.

                         TOM
          I am way too exhausted to deal with
          his shit.

                         KURTIS
          Don't listen to him he's probably
          just trying to get under your skin.

                         TOM
          Maybe you're right.

                         JOHN
          Did you guys hear about the
          assembly today?

                         TOM
              We have one today?

                         KURTIS
              Do you know what on.

Kurtis stands up and gets his bag ready and it tips over and
a picture falls out of a chubby fat kid and a young girl
high school age.

                         KURTIS
              Shit.

                         TOM
              That was smooth.

John picks up the picture to hand it to Kurtis.

                         JOHN
              Whoa who's the chubby kid and who's
              the girl?

Kurtis realizes it what John has and grabs it quick.

                         KURTIS
              It's nothing, from a while ago and
              very long story, so what's this
              assembly on.

Kurtis puts the rest of his stuff in his bag.

Kurtis starts to put his bag on.

                         JOHN
              Not sure, somebody named Rachel,
              Rachel's challenge or something
              like that.

Kurtis stops in his tracks.

                         KURTIS
              Really?

                         TOM
              Do you know it?

                         KURTIS
              You can say that, let's get to
              class though.

Tom, John and Kurtis leave the cafeteria.

INT HALLWAY/TOM'S LOCKER DAY.

Tom and John walk up to the locker.

Kurtis is at his locker across the hall.

>   JOHN
>   You don't have a lock on?

>   TOM
>   No, I lost it a while ago and I
>   just haven't tried to get a new one
>   yet.

>   JOHN
>   You're not worried about someone
>   taking your stuff?

>   TOM
>   Nah I don't keep anything in here
>   but my text book.

Tom opens the locker and looks in it.

Tom starts not being able to breathe

Tom begins to shake and feel like the room is spinning.

Tom looks at John in Terror trying to speak but unable to.

>   KURTIS
>   So what did he leave you? A bag of
>   dog crap or something?

>   JOHN
>   Tom?

Kurtis turns around to see Tom reaching out for John looking
very pale.

Tom falls against the lockers and slides to the floor.

Kurtis rushes over and kneels next to him.

>   KURTIS
>   Tom breathe man.

>   JOHN
>   (Panic in his voice)
>   What's wrong with him, why is He
>   breathing like that.

                         KURTIS
               John go get the nurse.

                         JOHN
               Is He going to be okay?

                         KURTIS
               John GO!

John runs off down the hall.

A crowd of students has noticed whats going on.

Glen is in the back smiling.

                         GLEN
               I told you I'd pay you back.

                         KURTIS
               Tom look at me man you have to take
               deep breathes.

Tom is shaking on the floor hyperventilating trying to
breath.

Tom is grasping his chest.

                         KURTIS
               You have to talk to me man, what
               happened.

Tom struggles to speak but just can't so he points to his
locker.

                         KURTIS
               You need something from your
               locker? What?

Tom shakes his head and just keeps pointing.

                         KURTIS
               Something in the locker did this to
               you?

Tom leans his head back and nearly passes out completely.

Kurtis shakes him

                         KURTIS
               Tom, come on man hang in there,
               Help is coming.

The crowd of kids is gasping in concern and watching.

(CONTINUED)

John and the Nurse come running down the hall with the
principal.

Kurtis steps back and lets the nurse check him.

> JOHN
> Did he say anything?

> KURTIS
> No He just kept pointing to his
> locker.

The nurse checks Tom out and checks his pupils.

> NURSE PRATT.
> He's in shock, we need to get him
> to the hospital.

> PRINCIPAL HOLLIS
> I've already called an Ambulance
> they should be here very soon.

Nurse Pratt feels Tom's hands and his head.

> NURSE PRATT.
> Jesus he's Ice cold, something
> scared the hell out of him.

> PRINCIPAL HOLLIS
> Kurtis what happened here?

> KURTIS
> Nothing we were going into our
> lockers before class and I turned
> around and he was pale white.

Kurtis spots Glen smiling and walking away.

> KURTIS
> Wait, Glen Thomas said he left a
> surprise in Tom's locker.

Kurtis and principal walk to the locker to look inside and
see Newspaper clippings and pictures of the wreck that
killed Tom's parents.

Kurtis grabs a note hanging on the front of all the
clippings it says "Enjoy the trip down memory lane"

paramedics arrive and cart Tom away with John following.

Kurtis hands the note to principal Hollis.

Kurtis walks off down the hall.

Everyone is still standing in the hall.

                    PRINCIPAL HOLLIS
          Alright everyone back to class
          shows over.

INT HOSPITAL ROOM DAY

Tom is laying in the hospital bed awake.

John comes around the corner and finds Tom.

Tom smiles and gives him a big wave.

                    TOM
          Yo, what's up bro, so glad to see
          ya.

                    JOHN
          Man are you alright? You scared the
          shit out of me.

Tom looks at himself then smiles.

                    TOM
          I feel great.

The nurse walks in to check on Tom.

                    NURSE RACHEL
          How are you feeling Tom?

                    TOM
          I feel amazing.

                    NURSE RACHEL
          That's really good.

                    JOHN
          Nurse? Why is he acting like that?

Rachel turns towards to John to talk to him.

                    NURSE RACHEL
          I gave him a Ativan.

                    JOHN
          Ativan?

                    NURSE RACHEL
          It's used to treat Anxiety, Tom had
          a very vicious episode.

Tom is making gestures to John about the nurse while she isn't looking.

                    JOHN
          Is he going to be alright?

                    NURSE RACHEL
          He should be, have him get plenty
          of rest, and He shouldn't drive.

                    JOHN
          I'll take him.

                    NURSE RACHEL
          Are you family?

                    JOHN
          Yes we're cousins.

                    TOM
          Nope, you're wrong John we are
          brothers.

                    JOHN
          He's lived with us since middle
          school so we're like brothers.

                    TOM
          We aren't like brothers we are, see
          that's what's been bothering me
          lately.

                    JOHN
          What?

                    TOM
          Your mom slept with my dad, he is
          your real father.

                    JOHN
          Wow that medication really messed
          you up.

                    TOM
          No dude I'm serious your mom lied
          to you, don't believe me look for
          yourself in her top drawer.

Nurse Rachel hands John some papers and a prescription.

                    NURSE RACHEL
          Just get this filled, It's diazepam
          in case he has another Anxiety
          attack.

                                                  (CONTINUED)

Tom stands up a little wobbly.

                    JOHN
          Come on let's go.

John helps Tom out the door.

Tom looks back at nurse Rachel.

                    TOM
          Hey, call me.

Tom winks at her.

INT. JOHN'S DINING ROOM AFTERNOON

John helps Tom to his seat who is still feeling sedated and
heavy headed.

John sets the prescription bag on the table.

                    JOHN
          Just sit there, I'll see if my mom
          is home.

                    TOM
          PSsst.

                    JOHN
          What?

                    TOM
          Top Drawer man, take a look.

John walks down the hall to his mom's room.

INT. CHARLOTTE'S ROOM DAY

John walks into the room

                    JOHN
          Mom are you home?

John looks around the empty room and looks at the Drawer.

John hesitates and turns to walk out but stops and looks
again.

                    JOHN
          Fuck it.

John walks over and puts his hand on the handle and takes a deep breath.

John opens the drawer and shuffles around some papers before taking out his birth certificate.

John has a mix of confusion and anger on his face, mostly confusion.

As John is trying to take it all in Charlotte walks in.

Charlotte's hand covers her mouth.

John and Charlotte stand there for a moment not saying anything.

                    JOHN
          What is this?

                    CHARLOTTE
          John Listen.

                    JOHN
          Because it looks like my Birth
          Certificate.

                    CHARLOTTE
          I can explain.

                    JOHN
          Explain?, Explain how you lied to
          me about knowing who my father us?

                    CHARLOTTE
          You don't understand, I wanted to
          tell you but I didn't know how.

                    JOHN
          HOW COULD YOU NOT TELL ME!

John throws the paper aside.

Charlotte flinches.

                    JOHN
          Holy shit Mom, me and Tom have been
          brothers this whole time, Did aunt
          Julie know?

                    CHARLOTTE
          No, and Tom's father made me swear
          to keep it a secret.

                         JOHN
               All this time. All this Fucking
               Time! You knew!

John slams his foot into the dresser.

                         JOHN
               I always thought my father
               abandoned me but he was right there
               the whole time.

Charlotte goes to put a hand on his shoulder

John bats it away angrily.

                         JOHN
               Don't fucking touch me, I think I'm
               going to be sick.

John gags and runs out of the room.

Charlotte starts crying and sinks to the floor.

INT JOHN'S DINING ROOM DAY

John comes storming down the hall

                         JOHN
               Come on man I need some fresh air.

                         TOM
               Hack it up?

                         JOHN
               Yup.

Tom stands up and throws on his Hoodie and wobbles out the
door.

John Slams the door behind him.

EXT JOHNS DRIVEWAY

Tom takes out the hacky Sack and tosses it to John.

John boots it hard into the air.

                         TOM
               I take it you looked in the drawer.

                         JOHN
          Yup.

                         TOM
          Sorry brother.

                         JOHN
          It's not like you lied to me my
          whole life.

Tom retrieves the hacky sack and the two kick it back and
forth for a bit.

                         JOHN
          I am so pissed off at her, I will
          never listen to her again.

                         TOM
          I'll never lead you wrong bro.

Kurtis Drives in and gets out.

                         KURTIS
          Tom are you alright?, dude That was
          some scary shit.

Tom gives him two thumbs up and smiles.

                         TOM
          Feel great now that they gave me a
          sedative.

                         JOHN
          Yeah I'm sure I will need one of
          those soon.

                         KURTIS
          Why? What's up?

                         TOM
          He just found out we're bros.

Kurtis looks confused.

                         JOHN
          Yeah like flesh and blood brothers,
          his father is my father.

                         KURTIS
          Wow.

                         TOM
               Yeah, pretty heavy huh?

                         KURTIS
               How did you find out?

                         JOHN
               I saw my birth certificate and I
               confronted my mom.

                         KURTIS
               That really sucks.

                         JOHN
               Yeah... you wanna hack?

                         KURTIS
               Sure.

The boys hack for a while.

                         TOM
               So How much trouble did that piece
               of shit get into?

Kurtis just looks at Tom.

                         TOM
               What? Tell me He got in some
               trouble.

                         KURTIS
               They claim that there is no proof
               He did it.

                         TOM
               UN-fucking believable, so that's it
               he just gets away with it?

                         KURTIS
               I know, all because his daddy is on
               the board, I guess we live in a
               world where you have to get justice
               yourself.

Kurtis's phone rings and he looks to see who it is.

                         KURTIS
               Damn, It's my dad I have to take
               this.

Kurtis walks away to talk for a minute then comes back.

                                              (CONTINUED)

                         KURTIS
          I Have to go home now guys but I'll
          come by tomorrow alright?

                         TOM
          Yeah that's cool man.

                         JOHN
          See ya later Kurtis.

                         KURTIS
          Hey, try and keep your head up
          guys, the both of you. Things will
          work out.

                         TOM
                    (coldly)
          Yeah, they will.

Kurtis drives off.

Tom just stands there

                         TOM
          I understand it now.

                         JOHN
          Understand what?

                         TOM
          My dream.

Tom smiles with a psychotic blank stare in his eyes.

                         TOM
          I have a plan. They'll all be
          punished.

                         JOHN
          What plan man.

Tom just turns and laughs and smiles at John.

                         TOM
          Just trust me, It's a good one.

INT. TOM/JOHN'S ROOM NIGHT

Tom is pacing back and forth explaining the end of his plan.

                                              (CONTINUED)

                         TOM
              And then that's when we jump in.

                         JOHN
              In a sick way that plan might work,
              but where would we get.

John stops talking because his mom is standing peering in
the doorway.

                         CHARLOTTE
              Just seeing if you boys need
              anything.

                         JOHN
              We don't

John gets up and shuts his door in his mom's face.

                         JOHN
              So like I was saying how would we
              get the stuff?

                         TOM
              Don't worry I have that covered,
              That kid frank.

                         JOHN
              The schitzo?

                         TOM
              Yeah He's perfect.

                         JOHN
              I don't know man doesn't this all
              seem like a little extreme.

                         TOM
              Extreme? There's no other choice
              John, They left me no choice and I
              see it so clear now.

                         JOHN
              I still don't know.

                         TOM
              We're brothers, You got my back
              don't you?

                         JOHN
              Yeah, I got your back.

                         TOM
               Don't even feel bad about this,
               They all have it coming.

                         JOHN
               I've never even fired a gun before.

                         TOM
               Dude how hard could it be, just
               point, aim and BOOM.

                         JOHN
               Alright, Tell me your plan one more
               time.

Tom claps his hands together.

                         TOM
               So you're in then? No backing out.

John takes a moment and just nods.

                         TOM
               Alright my brother, lets go to
               battle, Phase one is to get the
               Guns.

                         JOHN
               How are you going to do that?

                         TOM
               I think I have all figured out.

EXT JOHNS DRIVEWAY DAY

Tom and John are nervously waiting in the driveway.

John checks his watch.

                         JOHN
               Are you sure He's even going to
               show.

                         TOM
               Trust me he'll be here.

Frank pulls into the driveway.

                         TOM
               See I told you.

Frank gets out of the car and looks all around.

                                                   (CONTINUED)

                          TOM
                Did you bring it?

Frank Nods and pulls out two duffel bags from the backseat.

                          TOM
                Holy shit dude, where did you get
                all this.

                          FRANK
                My dads been preparing me for years
                warning me, he had this stock pile.

                          TOM
                Where is he now?

                          FRANK
                Prison.

                          JOHN
                What did he do?

                          FRANK
                His only crime was he knew too
                much, He got too close to exposing
                the truth.

                          TOM
                What truth?

Frank looks all around and see's Kurtis's car coming and
quickly jumps in his.

                          TOM
                Wait you remember the plan for
                tomorrow right?

Frank just nods.

                          TOM
                Don't you need a weapon?

                          FRANK
                I got plenty more where that stash
                came from.

Frank backs out very quickly.

Kurtis pulls in as Frank pulls out and away.

                          JOHN
                The truth? a huge stash of ammo,
                who is his father Fox Mulder.

                                            (CONTINUED)

                              TOM
                    I don't know but I sure am glad
                    he's not an enemy.

                              JOHN
                    Yeah no kidding.

Kurtis walks over to them and puts his bag on the ground.

                              KURTIS
                    Hey guys, How's it going?

                              TOM
                    It's going good man.

                              KURTIS
                    Was that Frank I saw pull out of
                    here?

                              JOHN
                    Yeah, He came over to drop off
                    some.

John looks at Tom.

                              KURTIS
                    Some what? what's in the bags?

                              TOM
                    Supplies.

                              KURTIS
                    Supplies for what.

                              TOM
                    Wanna see them?

                              KURTIS
                    Yeah sure.

Tom reaches in the bag and pulls out a 9mm and points it at
Kurtis.

Kurtis ducks for cover.

                              KURTIS
                    Dude what the fuck is that.

                              TOM
                    My justice.

                         KURTIS
               Tom what are you talking about, get
               that gun out of my face.

                         TOM
               Bang.

Kurtis flinches

Tom lowers the gun.

                         TOM
               Relax I'd never shoot you, plus
               it's not even loaded.

                         KURTIS
               Why do you have a bunch of guns

                         TOM
               They have to pay.

                         KURTIS
               Who?

                         TOM
               Just don't get in my way Kurtis.

                         KURTIS
               Tom come on this isn't the answer.

                         TOM
               It goes down tomorrow at Noon, tell
               Katie to stay home too. I don't
               want you two to get hurt.

                         KURTIS
               John you can't tell me you are in
               on this.

John shows some doubt in his eyes and Tom interrupts him.

                         TOM
               John is my brother he has my back
               to the end right John?

                         JOHN
               Yeah, til the end.

                         KURTIS
               This is insane, I know your upset
               but.

                                TOM
                    But what? I'm sick of being pushed
                    down, I am getting my own justice.

Tom loads a clip into the pistol and cocks it.

                                TOM
                    Get out of here Kurtis, and do not
                    try to stop me.

Kurtis puts his hand up and slowly backs to his car and
leaves.

                                JOHN
                    Do you think that was smart man,
                    what if he tells.

                                TOM
                    He won't. Here help me bring this
                    all inside.

INT. TOM/JOHN'S ROOM NIGHT

Cue emotional music.

John is playing roller coaster Tycoon on his computer

Tom is writing in his journal.

John's mom is looking in from the hallway.

John looks up at his mom and then away.

Charlotte tears up and walks away.

INT KURTIS'S ROOM NIGHT

Kurtis is sitting on his bed looking through pictures of him
and Katie and a young picture of himself standing with a
young female.

Kurtis puts the picture down and texts Katie he loves her.

Kurtis looks at his history book but sighs and puts his book
aside.

Kurtis grabs the picture of him and the girl from when he
was younger.

                         KURTIS
           I wish you were here to tell me
           what I should do.

Kurtis leans back and peers out the window.

INT. TOM/JOHN'S ROOM NIGHT

Tom finishes writing in his Journal and puts it in a manilla
envelope with a note asking Charlotte to deliver this
tomorrow.

Tom lays his head on his pillow and drifts off to sleep.

INT KURTIS'S ROOM NIGHT

Kurtis is still laying there when his phone rings.

                         KURTIS
           Hey hon.

                         KATIE
           Hi.

                         KURTIS
           Look I'm sorry things have been
           rough between us.

                         KATIE
           No I'm sorry I've just been scared
           and I wish you were with me
           tonight.

                         KURTIS
           You know what I can't stop thinking
           about tonight?

                         KATIE
           No, what?

                         KURTIS
           Our first kiss.

                         KATIE
           Remind me.

                         KURTIS
           I remember how nervous I was, you
           were in that hot pink Bikini on
           July 4th. Mmm Best holiday ever.

                    KATIE
          That really was a fun day wasn't
          it?

                    KURTIS
          It is one of my favorite memories.
          That and of course our camping trip
          this summer.

                    KATIE
          Yeah I remember that as well, I got
          covered in mosquito bites because
          someone didn't zip the tent all the
          way.

Kurtis Laughs.

                    KURTIS
          Can't deny it was a memorable first
          time.

                    KATIE
          Yeah, Listen I have to tell you
          something.

Kurtis Interrupts her

                    KURTIS
          Don't go to school tomorrow.

                    KATIE
          Why?

                    KURTIS
          Just trust me and promise me no
          matter what you won't go to school
          tomorrow.

                    KATIE
          You're scaring me.

                    KURTIS
          I can't tell you why I just have a
          really bad feeling.

                    KATIE
          Okay I promise but I have something
          to tell you.

                    KURTIS
          Save it for tomorrow, and I have
          something to tell you now tonight.

                         KATIE
              What's that.

                         KURTIS
              That I have always and will always
              love you no matter what happens.

                         KATIE
              You have no idea how much that
              means to me right now.

                         KURTIS
              We will talk tomorrow, I promise.

                         KATIE
              Alright, goodnight I love you.

Kurtis Smiles and closes the phone.

Kurtis leans back in his bed and sighs deeply.

INT DR. HARRIS OFFICE MORNING

Tom walks in with his journal sealed in a envelope and
slides it under Dr. Harris' door.

EXT SCHOOL PARKING LOT MORNING

Tom and John are sitting inside their car.

John opens his car door and throws up.

John wipes his mouth and shuts the door.

                         JOHN
              Dude I don't know if I can do this.

                         TOM
              Why?

                         JOHN
              I'm scared.

                         TOM
              I am too man, I threw up this
              morning but you have to man up.
              Don't puss out on me now.

Tom puts his hand on John's shoulder.

                                            (CONTINUED)

                              TOM
                    Hey Look at me bro.

John looks at Tom.

                              TOM
                    I need you on this, Are you with
                    me.

                              JOHN
                    Yeah.. Yeah I'm with you.

                              TOM
                    Good.

                              JOHN
                    I don't see Kurtis, maybe He took
                    your advice after all.

                              TOM
                    I hope so, well it's time let's go
                    in.

Tom and John get out of their car and put their backpacks on
that have the guns in them and they walk into the school.

INT. LIBRARY DAY

Tom walks in and sits at one of the tables.

Tom pulls out a notebook to make it look like he is working.

Tom looks all around him and up at the clock, It reads
11:55.

INT. CAFETERIA DAY

John is sitting at a table by himself, the students just
starting to pour in.

John tries to steady his shaking hand as he looks up at the
clock reading 11:55

John takes a deep breath.

INT DR. HARRIS OFFICE DAY

Dr. Harris sits down at his desk with the envelope and opens it.

INT. LIBRARY DAY

Tom is sitting there looking out to the window.

                    TOM
                (Voice Over)
          Dear Dr. Harris, I know you have
          wanted to see this for some time
          and It is time now. I want to thank
          you, I was broken when we met
          devastated and soaked in tragedy. I
          want you to know you really did
          help me. I have let them walk on me
          for far too long.

INT CAFETERIA DAY

John is sitting there very nervously watching the clock
which reads 11:58.

                    TOM
          My cousin, well brother actually I
          know will do anything for me. He
          too has been bullied. It turns out
          I'm a bully too, I used the fact
          that we were brothers to push him
          into helping me. He is a good kid,
          I can tell he doesn't want to do
          this but doesn't want to let me
          down.

INT. LIBRARY DAY

Tom sits there staring at the clock.

students file in library.

Mr. Platsberg and Glen walk in.

Tom's eyes remain set on the clock.

                    TOM
          I had a dream once, I told you
          about the beach and the darkness. I
          know what it means now, it's a
                (MORE)

(CONTINUED)

                    TOM (cont'd)
          choice between the right thing and
          wrong. To trust the system or Exact
          revenge. Well today I make my last
          stand, the system is flawed and
          doesn't work, Evil goes unpunished
          but today.. Today I will slay evil.

INT DR. HARRIS OFFICE DAY

Dr. Harris reads the journal in his chair.

                    TOM
          These will be my final words to you
          Dr. It all ends today, Today I will
          be the Judge and my bullets the
          jury. A fair and just ending. When
          the police come they will kill me
          but at least I'll know today I took
          a stand when no one would stand for
          me. Goodbye Dr. and please remember
          none of it was your fault.

INT. LIBRARY DAY

Tom can hear nothing but the clock and his own heart beat
staring at the second hand.

The second ticks to 12:00 then silence.

INT. CAFETERIA DAY

John Looks at the clock as it hits noon and slowly reaches
for his bag and the gun.

INT SCHOOL FRONT LOBBY DAY

Silently Frank walks in Loaded with a hunting rifle past the
office.

The office ladies scream and drop behind their desk.

Frank fires a round high into the office not hitting anyone.

a voice comes over the loudspeaker

                    PRINCIPAL HOLLIS
          This is a lock-down, we have a
          intruder inside the building, this
                    (MORE)

                              PRINCIPAL HOLLIS (cont'd)
                    is not a drill, I repeat this is
                    not a drill.

INT CAFETERIA DAY

Kids pile into the Cafeteria and a teacher shuts the lights
down and locks the door.

John stands up and pulls a Mac-11 out aiming it to the
unsuspecting crowd and fires hitting several students.

INT. LIBRARY DAY

Tom stands up and Pulls the 9mm out and cocks it.

                              TOM
                    You will all be judged and punished
                    starting with you Glen.

Tom walks over to him quickly his gun aimed.

Glen puts his hands up.

                              GLEN
                    Dude, dude don't I'm.. I'm

                              TOM
                    You are what? huh? Sorry? No you
                    are not.

                              GLEN
                    I didn't mean it. Please stop I'm
                    begging you don't do this.

                              TOM
                    Did you stop when I was telling you
                    to stop picking on me and my
                    cousin.

                              GLEN
                    I...I..

                              TOM
                    Who's the pussy now. Beg for your
                    life.

                              GLEN
                    Please, I'm Begging you don't.

Tom fires 4 rounds into Glens chest sending him to the
ground bleeding out.

Tom turns to the screaming crowd.

>   TOM
>   (screaming)
>   Shut up! All of you. You are all as
>   guilty as him. You stood by and Did
>   nothing.

>   MR. PLATSBERG
>   Just put the gun down son.

>   TOM
>   Oh fuck you, you might be more
>   guilty then some.

>   MR. PLATSBERG
>   Let's talk about this.

>   TOM
>   No, I'm done talking.

Tom fires 2 rounds into Mr. Platsberg's head killing him
instantly.

While shooting Tom accidentally puts the safety on.

He takes his eyes off the crowd to fix the gun.

Students scatter for the door running out into the hall

Tom Chases them.

INT HALLWAY DAY

Tom fires at the fleeing students.

The students run in terror.

Tom reloads the gun with another clip.

>   KURTIS
>   Tom stop!

Tom slowly turns around.

>   TOM
>   I told you not to be here.

>   KURTIS
>   I couldn't let you do this Tom.

                              TOM
                    It has to be done, Don't you see
                    that. They have to be punished.

Kurtis steps towards Tom

Tom raises the gun at Kurtis.

                              TOM
                    Stop right there!

                              KURTIS
                    Alright, Alright. Tom you have to
                    know this isn't the answer.

                              TOM
                    They were guilty.

                              KURTIS
                    Glen was yes but this isn't
                    justice, and what about the other
                    people you've hurt that are
                    innocent. They have done nothing.

                              TOM
                    That's right! they stood by and
                    watched and laughed and they did
                    nothing, as far as I'm concerned
                    they're as guilty too.

Tom's eyes start to water, Distant gunshots go off.

                              KURTIS
                    Do you remember that picture I had
                    of that fat kid standing next to a
                    girl.

                              TOM
                    Yeah?

                              KURTIS
                    It was me, I'm the fat kid. Do you
                    want to know who the girl is?

                              TOM
                    Okay.

                              KURTIS
                    Her name was Rachel, She helped at
                    my middle school's plays and she
                    was nice to me.

                        TOM
            Where is she now?

                        KURTIS
            She died because two kids she had
            never picked on decided to take
            matters into their own hands. She
            was just eating her lunch when she
            was killed.

Tom starts to lower the weapon

Kurtis gets close enough to put his hand on the gun to start
lowering it.

                        KURTIS
            Just put it down man, you can still
            come out of this.

INT OUTSIDE THE CAFETERIA DAY

A fully armed swat team has entered the school.

The Swat team comes around the corner to find Frank aiming
at them.

A swat member takes him down.

They reach the cafeteria and open the door guns drawn at
John.

Officer Connolly is with the group and Attempts to talk John
down.

                        JOHN
            Get back or I'll shoot.

                        OFFICER CONNOLLY
            Put the Gun down now and we can all
            walk away from this.

                        JOHN
            There is no walking away from this,
            after what I've done.

John starts shaking violently and looks at the gun then at
officer Connolly.

                        OFFICER CONNOLLY
            There is still a way out John.

John thinks for a minute and looks down again and all
around.

                                            (CONTINUED)

                    JOHN
          You're right.

John reaches and pulls the gun up toward the SWAT team.

The SWAT Team fires at him killing him.

John's body falls to the floor.

Officer Connolly Runs for the second floor where Tom is.

INT HALLWAY DAY

Tom hears the shot go off downstairs and it scares him.

Tom accidentally squeezes the trigger and looks at Kurtis in
horror.

Kurtis looks at him in shock.

                    TOM
          Oh my god Kurtis, I'm so sorry.

Kurtis stumbles backwards and falls to the floor still
alive.

Tom starts crying and drops to his knees.

                    TOM
          I didn't mean to do that.

Tom looks just passed Kurtis and see's his parents.

                    MRS. LEWISTON
          It's all going to be alright Tom.

                    MR. LEWISTON
          It's over son, time to rest.

                    MRS. LEWISTON
          Dry your tears honey.

Kurtis looks behind him and sees nothing.

Tom wipes his eyes.

                    TOM
          Alright mom, I'm coming

Tom raises the gun to his head.

Officer Connolly comes rushing up the stairs.

                                        (CONTINUED)

                    OFFICER CONNOLLY
          Tom No!

Tom fires a round into his head killing himself.

Officer Connolly rushes over to check Kurtis.

                    OFFICER CONNOLLY
          Hang in there Kurtis, you're going
          to be alright you hear me.

Kurtis's phone rings and goes to voice mail.

                    KATIE
              (Voice over)
          Kurtis I, I wanted to wait until I
          knew for sure but I took a test
          today and I'm pregnant. I'm really
          scared and I need you right now.

The sounds of school start fading to Kurtis, He flashes
through memories with Katie, Their first kiss on the beach
and the camping trip that summer where they made love for
the first time.

                    OFFICER CONNOLLY
          Hey just hang in their Kurtis stay
          with me.

Kurtis smiles

Paramedics arrive to treat Kurtis and the other students.

EXT. SOCCER FIELD EARLY MORNING

Students are sitting in Caps and Gowns in the folded seats
placed there.

Principal Hollis is Calling names.

                    PRINCIPAL HOLLIS
          Katie Caron

Katie walks up to accept her diploma shaking the principal's
hands and looking at the crowd.

Katie waves to her parents and her baby.

Kurtis waves at her and then motions toward the exit.

Kurtis walks away.

Katie runs to her parents after the ceremony and hugs her
baby girl.

                    KATIES MOM
          Congratulations sweetheart, We're
          so proud of you.

                    KATIES DAD
          Congratulations.

Katie hugs her crying mom and her dad.

                    KATIE
          Thank you guys, aww don't cry. I
          love you both but now I'm going to
          see Kurtis.

                    KATIES MOM
          Alright sweetie.

Katie takes the baby and walks away

Katie's parents exchange sad looks.

INT.BEACH AREA DAY

Katie walks up with the baby to Kurtis standing by the tree
and water.

                    KURTIS
          Hey Beautiful, you are a sight for
          sore eyes.

                    KATIE
          I could feel you there today.

                    KURTIS
          Of course I was there I wouldn't
          miss it for the world.

                    KATIE
          This is our little baby Ta-suil, It
          means hope.

                    KURTIS
          I love it, she's perfect.

                    KATIE
          I miss you Kurtis and I'll make
          sure our little girl knows how good
          of a man you were.

Katie kneels down revealing a white cross with Kurtis's name
and date of birth on it.

Katie kisses the marker.

                    KATIE
          I know this is the spot where we
          had our first kiss so I spread some
          of your ashes here. I'll never
          forget you Kurtis.

                    KURTIS
          I'll always be in your heart.

Katie stands up and walks away tears in her eyes.

                    KURTIS
          My sweet baby girl, a true
          statement that through the darkest
          ashes of tragedy can still rise
          just a little hope. I and a few
          others lost our lives that day to
          senseless school violence, I pray
          we are the last.

        ....THE END......................

Made in the USA
Middletown, DE
01 October 2016